Lecture Notes in Computer Science 8059

Commenced Publication in 1973
Founding and Former Series Editors:
Gerhard Goos, Juris Hartmanis, and Jan van Leeuwen

T0172207

Abdelkader Hameurlain   Wenny Rahayu
David Taniar (Eds.)

Data Management in Cloud, Grid and P2P Systems

6th International Conference, Globe 2013
Prague, Czech Republic, August 28-29, 2013
Proceedings

 Springer

Volume Editors

Abdelkader Hameurlain
Paul Sabatier University
IRIT Institut de Recherche en Informatique de Toulouse
118, route de Narbonne, 31062 Toulouse Cedex, France
E-mail: hameur@irit.fr

Wenny Rahayu
La Trobe University
Department of Computer Science and Computer Engineering
Melbourne, VIC 3086, Australia
E-mail: w.rahayu@latrobe.edu.au

David Taniar
Monash University
Clayton School of Information Technology
Clayton, VIC 3800, Australia
E-mail: dtaniar@gmail.com

ISSN 0302-9743   e-ISSN 1611-3349
ISBN 978-3-642-40052-0   e-ISBN 978-3-642-40053-7
DOI 10.1007/978-3-642-40053-7
Springer Heidelberg Dordrecht London New York

Library of Congress Control Number: 2013944289

CR Subject Classification (1998): H.2, C.2, I.2, H.3

LNCS Sublibrary: SL 3 – Information Systems and Application, incl. Internet/Web
and HCI

Typesetting: Camera-ready by author, data conversion by Scientific Publishing Services, Chennai, India

Printed on acid-free paper

Springer is part of Springer Science+Business Media (www.springer.com)

Preface

Globe is now an established conference on data management in cloud, grid and peer-to-peer systems. These systems are characterized by high heterogeneity, high autonomy and dynamics of nodes, decentralization of control and large-scale distribution of resources. These characteristics bring new dimensions and difficult challenges to tackling data management problems. The still open challenges to data management in cloud, grid and peer-to-peer systems are multiple, such as scalability, elasticity, consistency, data storage, security and autonomic data management.

The 6th International Conference on Data Management in Grid and P2P Systems (Globe 2013) was held during August 28–29, 2013, in Prague, Czech Republic. The Globe Conference provides opportunities for academics and industry researchers to present and discuss the latest data management research and applications in cloud, grid and peer-to-peer systems.

Globe 2013 received 19 papers from 11 countries. The reviewing process led to the acceptance of 10 papers for presentation at the conference and inclusion in this LNCS volume. Each paper was reviewed by at least three Program Committee members. The selected papers focus mainly on data management (e.g., data partitioning, storage systems, RDF data publishing, querying linked data, consistency), MapReduce applications, and virtualization.

The conference would not have been possible without the support of the Program Committee members, external reviewers, members of the DEXA Conference Organizing Committee, and the authors. In particular, we would like to thank Gabriela Wagner and Roland Wagner (FAW, University of Linz) for their help in the realization of this conference.

June 2013

Abdelkader Hameurlain
Wenny Rahayu
David Taniar

Organization

Conference Program Chairpersons

Abdelkader Hameurlain IRIT, Paul Sabatier University, Toulouse,
France
David Taniar Clayton School of Information Technology,
Monash University, Clayton, Victoria,
Australia

Publicity Chair

Wenny Rahayu La Trobe University, Victoria, Australia

Program Committee

Philippe Balbiani IRIT, Paul Sabatier University, Toulouse,
France
Nadia Bennani LIRIS, INSA of Lyon, France
Djamal Benslimane LIRIS, Universty of Lyon, France
Lionel Brunie LIRIS, INSA of Lyon, France
Elizabeth Chang Digital Ecosystems & Business intelligence
Institute, Curtin University, Perth, Australia
Qiming Chen HP Labs, Palo Alto, California, USA,
Alfredo Cuzzocrea ICAR-CNR, University of Calabria, Italy
Frédéric Cuppens Telecom, Bretagne, France
Bruno Defude Telecom INT, Evry, France
Kayhan Erciyes Ege University, Izmir, Turkey
Shahram Ghandeharizadeh University of Southern California, USA
Tasos Gounaris Aristotle University of Thessaloniki, Greece
Farookh Hussain University of Technology Sydney (UTS),
Sydney, Australia
Sergio Ilarri University of Zaragoza, Spain
Ismail Khalil Johannes Kepler University, Linz, Austria
Gildas Menier LORIA, University of South Bretagne, France
Anirban Mondal University of Delhi, India
Riad Mokadem IRIT, Paul Sabatier University, Toulouse,
France

Franck Morvan	IRIT, Paul Sabatier University, Toulouse, France
Faïza Najjar	National Computer Science School, Tunis, Tunisia
Kjetil Nørvåg	Norwegian University of Science and Technology, Trondheim, Norway
Jean-Marc Pierson	IRIT, Paul Sabatier University, Toulouse, France
Claudia Roncancio	LIG, Grenoble University, France
Florence Sedes	IRIT, Paul Sabatier University, Toulouse, France
Fabricio A.B. Silva	Army Technological Center, Rio de Janeiro, Brazi
Mário J.G. Silva	University of Lisbon, Portugal
Hela Skaf	LINA, Nantes University, France
A. Min Tjoa	IFS, Vienna University of Technology, Austria
Farouk Toumani	LIMOS, Blaise Pascal University, France
Roland Wagner	FAW, University of Linz, Austria
Wolfram Wöß	FAW, University of Linz, Austria

External Reviewers

Christos Doulkeridis	University of Piraeus, Greece
Franck Ravat	IRIT, Paul Sabatier University, Toulouse, France
Raquel Trillo	University of Zaragoza, Spain
Shaoyi Yin	IRIT, Paul Sabatier University, Toulouse, France

Table of Contents

Data Partitioning and Consistency

Data Partitioning for Minimizing Transferred Data in MapReduce 1
Miguel Liroz-Gistau, Reza Akbarinia, Divyakant Agrawal,
Esther Pacitti, and Patrick Valduriez

Incremental Algorithms for Selecting Horizontal Schemas of Data
Warehouses: The Dynamic Case 13
Ladjel Bellatreche, Rima Bouchakri, Alfredo Cuzzocrea, and
Sofian Maabout

Scalable and Fully Consistent Transactions in the Cloud through
Hierarchical Validation 26
Jon Grov and Peter Csaba Ölveczky

RDF Data Publishing, Querying Linked Data, and Applications

A Distributed Publish/Subscribe System for RDF Data 39
Laurent Pellegrino, Fabrice Huet, Françoise Baude, and
Amjad Alshabani

An Algorithm for Querying Linked Data Using Map-Reduce 51
Manolis Gergatsoulis, Christos Nomikos, Eleftherios Kalogeros, and
Matthew Damigos

Effects of Network Structure Improvement on Distributed RDF
Querying 63
Liaquat Ali, Thomas Janson, Georg Lausen, and
Christian Schindelhauer

Deploying a Multi-interface RESTful Application in the Cloud 75
Erik Albert and Sudarshan S. Chawathe

Distributed Storage Systems and Virtualization

Using Multiple Data Stores in the Cloud: Challenges and Solutions 87
Rami Sellami and Bruno Defude

Repair Time in Distributed Storage Systems...................... 99
   Frédéric Giroire, Sandeep Kumar Gupta, Remigiusz Modrzejewski,
   Julian Monteiro, and Stéphane Perennes

Development and Evaluation of a Virtual PC Type Thin Client
System 111
   Katsuyuki Umezawa, Tomoya Miyake, and Hiromi Goto

Author Index... 125

Data Partitioning for Minimizing Transferred Data in MapReduce

Miguel Liroz-Gistau[1], Reza Akbarinia[1], Divyakant Agrawal[2],
Esther Pacitti[3], and Patrick Valduriez[1]

[1] INRIA & LIRMM, Montpellier, France
{Miguel.Liroz_Gistau,Reza.Akbarinia,Patrick.Valduriez}@inria.fr
[2] University of California, Santa Barbara
agrawal@cs.ucsb.edu
[3] University Montpellier 2, INRIA & LIRMM, Montpellier, France
Esther.Pacitti@lirmm.fr

Abstract. Reducing data transfer in MapReduce's shuffle phase is very important because it increases data locality of reduce tasks, and thus decreases the overhead of job executions. In the literature, several optimizations have been proposed to reduce data transfer between mappers and reducers. Nevertheless, all these approaches are limited by how intermediate key-value pairs are distributed over map outputs. In this paper, we address the problem of high data transfers in MapReduce, and propose a technique that repartitions tuples of the input datasets, and thereby optimizes the distribution of key-values over mappers, and increases the data locality in reduce tasks. Our approach captures the relationships between input tuples and intermediate keys by monitoring the execution of a set of MapReduce jobs which are representative of the workload. Then, based on those relationships, it assigns input tuples to the appropriate chunks. We evaluated our approach through experimentation in a Hadoop deployment on top of Grid5000 using standard benchmarks. The results show high reduction in data transfer during the shuffle phase compared to Native Hadoop.

1 Introduction

MapReduce [4] has established itself as one of the most popular alternatives for big data processing due to its programming model simplicity and automatic management of parallel execution in clusters of machines. Initially proposed by Google to be used for indexing the web, it has been applied to a wide range of problems having to process big quantities of data, favored by the popularity of Hadoop [2], an open-source implementation. MapReduce divides the computation in two main phases, namely map and reduce, which in turn are carried out by several tasks that process the data in parallel. Between them, there is a phase, called shuffle, where the data produced by the map phase is ordered, partitioned and transferred to the appropriate machines executing the reduce phase.

A. Hameurlain, W. Rahayu, and D. Taniar (Eds.): Globe 2013, LNCS 8059, pp. 1–12, 2013.

MapReduce applies the principle of "moving computation towards data" and thus tries to schedule map tasks in MapReduce executions close to the input data they process, in order to maximize data locality. Data locality is desirable because it reduces the amount of data transferred through the network, and this reduces energy consumption as well as network traffic in data centers.

Recently, several optimizations have been proposed to reduce data transfer between mappers and reducers. For example, [5] and [10] try to reduce the amount of data transferred in the shuffle phase by scheduling reduce tasks close to the map tasks that produce their input. Ibrahim et al. [7] go even further and dynamically partition intermediate keys in order to balance load among reduce tasks and decrease network transfers. Nevertheless, all these approaches are limited by how intermediate key-value pairs are distributed over map outputs. If the data associated to a given intermediate key is present in all map outputs, even if we assign it to a reducer executing in the same machine, the rest of the pairs still have to be transferred.

In this paper, we propose a technique, called MR-Part, that aims at minimizing the transferred data between mappers and reducers in the shuffle phase of MapReduce. MR-Part captures the relationships between input tuples and intermediate keys by monitoring the execution of a set of MapReduce jobs which are representative of the workload. Then, based on the captured relationships, it partitions the input files, and assigns input tuples to the appropriate fragments in such a way that subsequent MapReduce jobs following the modeled workload will take full advantage of data locality in the reduce phase. In order to characterize the workload, we inject a monitoring component in the MapReduce framework that produces the required metadata. Then, another component, which is executed offline, combines the information captured for all the MapReduce jobs of the workload and partitions the input data accordingly. We have modeled the workload by means of an hypergraph, to which we apply a min-cut k-way graph partitioning algorithm to assign the tuples to the input fragments.

We implemented MR-Part in Hadoop, and evaluated it through experimentation on top of Grid5000 using standard benchmarks. The results show significant reduction in data transfer during the shuffle phase compared to Native Hadoop. They also exhibit a significant reduction in execution time when network bandwidth is limited.

This paper is organized as follows: In Section 2, we briefly describe MapReduce, and then define formally the problem we address. In Section 3, we propose MR-Part. In Section 4, we report the results of our experimental tests evaluating its efficiency. Section 5 presents the related work and Section 6 concludes.

2 Problem Definition

2.1 MapReduce Background

MapReduce is a programming model based on two primitives, $map : (K_1, V_1) \rightarrow list(K_2, V_2)$ and $reduce : (K_2, list(V_1)) \rightarrow list(K_3, V_3)$. The map function processes key/value pairs and produces a set of intermediate/value pairs. Intermediate key/value pairs are merged and sorted based on the intermediate key k_2 and provided as input to the reduce function.

MapReduce jobs are executed over a distributed system composed of a master and a set of workers. The input is divided into several splits and assigned to map tasks. The master schedules map tasks in the workers by taking into account data locality (nodes holding the assigned input are preferred).

The output of the map tasks is divided into as many partitions as reducers are scheduled in the system. Entries with the same intermediate key k_2 should be assigned to the same partition to guarantee the correctness of the execution. All the intermediate key/value pairs of a given partition are sorted and sent to the worker where the corresponding reduce task is going to be executed. This phase is called shuffle. Default scheduling of reduce task does not take into consideration any data locality constraint. As a consequence, depending on how intermediate keys appear in the input splits and how the partitioning is done, the amount of data that has to be transferred through the network in the shuffle phase may be significant.

2.2   Problem Statement

We are given a set of MapReduce jobs which are representative of the system workload, and a set of input files. We assume that future MapReduce jobs follow similar patterns as those of the representative workload, at least in the generation of intermediate keys.

The goal of our system is to automatically partition the input files so that the amount of data that is transferred through the network in the shuffle phase is minimized in future executions. We make no assumptions about the scheduling of map and reduce tasks, and only consider intelligent partitioning of intermediate keys to reducers, e.g., as it is done in [7].

Let us formally state the problem which we address. Let the input data for a MapReduce job, job_α, be composed of a set of data items $D = \{d_1, ..., d_n\}$ and divided into a set of chunks $C = \{C_1, ..., C_p\}$. Function $loc : D \rightarrow C$ assigns data items to chunks. Let job_α be composed of $M_\alpha = \{m_1, ..., m_p\}$ map tasks and $R_\alpha = \{r_1, ..., r_q\}$ reduce tasks. We assume that each map task m_i processes chunk c_i. Let $N_\alpha = \{n_1, .., n_s\}$ be the set of machines used in the job execution; $node(t)$ represents the machine where task t is executed.

Let $I_\alpha = \{i_1, .., i_m\}$ be the set of intermediate key-value pairs produced by the map phase, such that $map(d_j) = \{i_{j_1}, ..., i_{j_t}\}$. $k(i_j)$ represents the key of intermediate pair i_j and $size(i_j)$ represents its total size in bytes. We define $output(m_i) \subseteq I_\alpha$ as the set of intermediate pairs produced by map task m_i, $output(m_i) = \bigcup_{d_j \in C_i} map(d_j)$. We also define $input(r_i) \subseteq I_\alpha$ as the set of intermediate pairs assigned to reduce task r_i. Function $part : k(I_\alpha) \rightarrow R$ assigns intermediate keys to reduce tasks.

Let i_j be an intermediate key-value pair, such that $i_j \in output(m)$ and $i_j \in input(r)$. Let $P_{i_j} \in \{0,1\}$ be a variable that is equal to 0 if intermediate pair i_j

is produced in the same machine where it is processed by the reduce task, and 1 otherwise, i.e., $P(i_j) = 0$ iff $node(m) = node(r)$.

Let $W = \{job_1, ..., job_w\}$ be the set of jobs in the workload. Our goal is to find loc and $part$ functions in a way in which $\sum_{job_\alpha \in W} \sum_{i_j \in I_\alpha} size(i_j)P(i_j)$ is minimized.

3   MR-Part

In this section, we propose MR-Part, a technique that by automatic partitioning of MapReduce input files allows Hadoop to take full advantage of locality-aware scheduling for reduce tasks, and to reduce significantly the amount of data transferred between map and reduce nodes during the shuffle phase. MR-Part proceeds in three main phases, as shown in Fig. 1: 1) Workload characterization, in which information about the workload is obtained from the execution of MapReduce jobs, and then combined to create a model of the workload represented as a hypergraph; 2) Repartitioning, in which a graph partitioning algorithm is applied over the hypergraph produced in the first phase, and based on the results the input files are repartitioned; 3) Scheduling, that takes advantage of the input partitioning in further executions of MapReduce jobs, and by an intelligent assignment of reduce tasks to the workers reduces the amount of data transferred in the shuffle phase. Phases 1 and 2 are executed offline over the model of the workload, so their cost is amortized over future job executions.

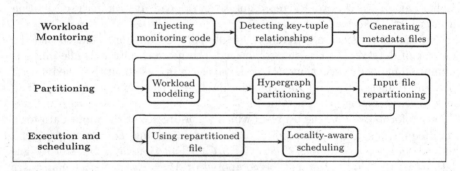

Fig. 1. MR-Part workflow scheme

3.1   Workload Characterization

In order to minimize the amount of data transferred through the network between map and reduce tasks, MR-Part tries to perform the following actions: 1) grouping all input tuples producing a given intermediate key in the same chunk and 2) assigning the key to a reduce task executing in the same node.

The first action needs to find the relationship between input tuples and intermediate keys. With that information, tuples producing the same intermediate key are co-located in the same chunk.

Monitoring. We inject a monitoring component in the MapReduce framework that monitors the execution of map tasks and captures the relationship between input tuples and intermediate keys. This component is completely transparent to the user program.

The development of the monitoring component was not straightforward because the map tasks receive entries of the form (K_1, V_1), but with this information alone we are not able to uniquely identify the corresponding input tuples. However, if we always use the same `RecordReader`[1] to read the file, we can uniquely identify an input tuple by a combination of its input file name, its chunk starting offset and the position of `RecordReader` when producing the input pairs for the map task.

For each map task, the monitoring component produces a metadata file as follows. When a new input chunk is loaded, the monitoring component creates a new metadata file and writes the chunk information (file name and starting offset). Then, it initiates a record counter (rc). Whenever an input pair is read, the counter is incremented by one. Moreover, if an intermediate key k is produced, it generates a pair (k, rc). When the processing of the input chunk is finished, the monitoring component groups all key-counter pairs by their key, and for each key it stores an entry of the form $\langle k, \{rc_1, ..., rc_n\} \rangle$ in the metadata file.

Combination. While executing a monitored job, all metadata is stored locally. Whenever a repartitioning is launched by the user, the information from different metadata files have to be combined in order to generate a hypergraph for each input file. The hypergraph is used for partitioning the tuples of an input file, and is generated by using the matadata files created in the monitoring phase.

A hypergraph $H = (H_V, H_E)$ is a generalization of a graph in which each hyper edge $e \in H_E$ can connect more than two vertices. In fact, a hyper edge is a subset of vertices, $e \subseteq H_V$. In our model, vertices represent input tuples and hyper edges characterize tuples producing the same intermediate key in a job.

The pseudo-code for generating the hypergraph is shown in Algorithm 1. Initially the hypergraph is empty, and new vertices and edges are added to it as the metadata files are read. The metadata of each job is processed separately. For each job, our algorithm creates a data structure T, which stores for each generated intermediate key, the set of input tuples that produce the key. For every entry in the file, the algorithm generates the corresponding tuple ids and adds them to the entry in T corresponding to the generated key. For easy id generation, we store in each metadata file, the number of input tuples processed for the associated chunk, n_i. We use the function $generateTupleID(c_i, rc) = \sum_{j=1}^{i-1} n_i + rc$ to translate record numbers into ids. After processing all metadata of a job, for each read tuple, our algorithm adds a vertex in the hypergraph (if it is not there). Then, for each intermediate key, it adds a hyper edge containing the set of tuples that have produced the key.

---

[1] The `RecordReader` is the component of MapReduce that parses the input and produce input key-value pairs. Normally each file format is parsed by a single `RecordReader`; therefore, using the same `RecordReader` for the same file is a common practice.

Algorithm 1. Metadata combination

Data: F: Input file; W: Set of jobs composing the workload
Result: $H = (H_V, H_E)$: Hypergraph modeling the workload
begin
    $H_E \leftarrow \emptyset$; $H_V \leftarrow \emptyset$
    foreach $job \in |W|$ **do**
        $T \leftarrow \emptyset$; $K \leftarrow \emptyset$
        foreach $m_i \in M_{job}$ **do**
            $md_i \leftarrow getMetadata(m_i)$
            if $F = getFile(md_i)$ **then**
                foreach $\langle k, \{rc_1, ..., rc_n\} \rangle \in md_i$ **do**
                    $\{t_1.id, ..., t_n.id\} \leftarrow generateTupleID(c_i, \{rc_1, ..., rc_n\})$
                    $T[k] \leftarrow T[k] \cup \{t_1.id, ..., t_n.id\}$; $K \leftarrow K \cup \{k\}$

        foreach $intermediate\ key\ k \in K$ **do**
            $H_V \leftarrow H_V \cup T[k]$; $H_E \leftarrow H_E \cup \{T[k]\}$

3.2 Repartitioning

Once we have modeled the workload of each input file through a hypergraph, we apply a min-cut k-way graph partitioning algorithm. The algorithm takes as input a value k and a hypergraph, and produces k disjoint subsets of vertices minimizing the sum of the weights of the edges between vertices of different subsets. Weights can be associated to vertices, for instance to represent different sizes. We set k as the number of chunks in the input file. By using the min-cut algorithm, the tuples that are used for generating the same intermediate key are usually assigned to the same partition.

The output of the algorithm indicates the set of tuples that have to be assigned to each of the input file chunks. Then, the input file should be repartitioned using the produced assignments. However, the file repartitioning cannot be done in a straightforward manner, particularly because the chunks are created by HDFS automatically as new data is appended to a file. We create a set of temporary files, one for each partition. Then, we read the original file, and for each read tuple, the graph algorithm output indicates to which of the temporary files the tuple should be copied. Then, two strategies are possible: 1) create a set of files in one directory, one per partition, as it is done in the reduce phase of MapReduce executions and 2) write the generated files sequentially in the same file. In both cases, at the end of the process, we remove the old file and rename the new file/directory to its name. The first strategy is straightforward and instead of writing data in temporary files, it can be written directly in HDFS. The second one has the advantage of not having to deal with more files but has to deal with the following issues:

- *Unfitted Partitions*: The size of partitions created by the partitioning algorithm may be different than the predefined chunk size, even if we set strict imbalance constraints in the algorithm. To approximate the chunk limits to the end of the temporary files when written one after the other, we can modify the order in which temporary files are written. We used a greedy approach in which we select at each time the temporary file whose size, added to the total size written, approximates the most to the next chunk limit.

- *Inappropriate Last Chunk*: The last chunk of a file is a special case, as its size is less than the predefined chunk size. However, the graph partitioning algorithm tries to make all partitions balanced and does not support such a constraint. In order to force one of the partitions to be of the size of the last chunk, we insert a virtual tuple, $t_{virtual}$, with the weight equivalent to the empty space in the last chunk. After discarding this tuple, one of the partitions would have a size proportional to the size of the last chunk.

The repartitioning algorithm's pseudo-code is shown in Algorithm 2. In the algorithm we represent RR as the `RecordReader` used to parse the input data. We need to specify the associated `RecordWriter`, here represented as RW, that performs the inverse function as RR. The reordering of temporary files is represented by the function $reorder()$.

Algorithm 2. Repartitioning

Data: F: Input file; $H = (H_V, H_E)$: Hypergraph modeling the workload; k: Number of partitions
Result: F': The repartitioned file
begin

    $H_V \leftarrow H_V \cup t_{virtual}$
    $\{P_1, ..., P_k\} \leftarrow mincut(H, k)$
    for $i \in (1, ..., k)$ **do**
        create $tempf_i$

    foreach $c_i \in F$ **do**
        $initialize(RR, c_i)$; $rc \leftarrow 0$
        while $t.data \leftarrow RR.next()$ **do**
            $t.id \leftarrow generateTupleID(c_i, rc)$
            $p \leftarrow getPartition(t.id, \{P_1, ..., P_k\})$
            $RW.write(tempf_p, t.data)$
            $rc \leftarrow rc + 1$

    $(j_1, ..., j_k) \leftarrow reorder(tempf_1, ..., tempf_k)$
    for $j \in (j_1, ..., j_k)$ **do**
        write $tempf_i$ in F'

The complexity of the algorithm is dominated by the min-cut algorithm execution. Min-cut graph partitioning is NP-Complete, however, several polynomial approximation algorithms have been developed for it. In this paper we use Pa-ToH[2] to partition the hypergraph. In the rest of the algorithm, an inner loop is executed n times, where n is the number of tuples. $generateTupleID()$ can be executed in $O(1)$ if we keep a table with n_i, the number of input tuples, for all input chunks. $getPartition()$ can also be executed in $O(1)$ if we keep an array storing for each tuple the assigned partition. Thus, the rest of the algorithm is done in $O(n)$.

---

[2] http://bmi.osu.edu/~umit/software.html

3.3   Reduce Tasks Locality-Aware Scheduling

In order to take advantage of the repartitioning, we need to maximize data locality when scheduling reduce tasks. We have adapted the algorithm proposed in [7], in which each (key,node) pair is given a fairness-locality score representing the ratio between the imbalance in reducers input and data locality when key is assigned to a reducer. Each key is processed independently in a greedy algorithm. For each key, candidate nodes are sorted by their key frequency in descending order (nodes with higher key frequencies have better data locality). But instead of selecting the node with the maximum frequency, further nodes are considered if they have a better fairness-locality score. The aim of this strategy is to balance reduce inputs as much as possible. On the whole, we made the following modifications in the MapReduce framework:

- The partitioning function is changed to assign a unique partition for each intermediate key.
- Map tasks, when finished, send to the master a list with the generated intermediate keys and their frequencies. This information is included in the Heartbeat message that is sent at task completion.
- The master assigns intermediate keys to the reduce tasks relying on this information in order to maximize data locality and to achieve load balancing.

3.4   Improving Scalability

Two strategies can be taken into account to improve the scalability of the presented algorithms: 1) the number of intermediate keys; 2) the size of the generated graph.

In order to deal with a high number of intermediate keys we have created the concept of virtual reducers, VR. Instead of using intermediate keys both in the metadata and the modified partitioning function we use k mod VR. Actually, this is similar to the way in which keys are assigned to reduce tasks in the original MapReduce, but in this case we set VR to a much greater number than the actual number of reducers. This decreases the amount of metadata that should be transferred to the master and the time to process the key frequencies and also the amount of edges that are generated in the hypergraph.

To reduce the number of vertices that should be processed in the graph partitioning algorithm, we perform a preparing step in which we coalesce tuples that always appear together in the edges, as they should be co-located together. The weights of the coalesced tuples would be the sum of the weights of the tuples that have been merged. This step can be performed as part of the combination algorithm that was described in Section 3.1.

4   Experimental Evaluation

In this section, we report the results of our experiments done for evaluating the performance of MR-Part. We first describe the experimental setup, and then present the results.

4.1 Set-Up

We have implemented MR-Part in Hadoop-1.0.4 and evaluated it on Grid5000 [1], a large scale infrastructure composed of different sites with several clusters of computers. In our experiments we have employed PowerEdge 1950 servers with 8 cores and 16 GB of memory. We installed Debian GNU/Linux 6.0 (squeeze) 64-bit in all nodes, and used the default parameters for Hadoop configuration.

We tested the proposed algorithm with queries from TPC-H, an ad-hoc decision support benchmark. Queries have been written in Pig [9][3], a dataflow system on top of Hadoop that translates queries into MapReduce jobs. Scale factor (which accounts for the total size of the dataset in GBs) and employed queries are specified on each specific test. After data population and data repartitioning the cluster is rebalanced in order to minimize the effects of remote transfers in the map phase.

As input data, we used lineitem, which is the biggest table in TPC-H dataset. In our tests, we used queries for which the shuffle phase has a significant impact in the total execution time. Particularly, we used the following queries: Q5 and Q9 that are examples of hash joins on different columns, Q7 that executes a replicated join and Q17 that executes a co-group. Note that, for any query data locality will be at least that of native Hadoop.

We compared the performance of MR-Part with that of native Hadoop (NAT) and reduce locality-aware scheduling (RLS) [7], which corresponds to changes explained in Section 3.3 but over the non-repartitioned dataset. We measured the percentage of transferred data in the shuffle phase for different queries and cluster sizes. We also measured the response time and shuffle time of MapReduce jobs under varying network bandwidth configurations.

4.2 Results

Transferred Data for Different Query Types. We repartitioned the dataset by using the metadata information collected from monitoring query executions. Then, we measured the amount of transferred data in the shuffled phase for our queries in the repartitioned dataset. Fig 2(a) depicts the percentage of data transferred for each of the queries on a 5 nodes cluster and scale factor of 5. As we can see, transferred data is around 80% in non repartitioned data sets (actually the data locality is always around 1 divided by the number of nodes for the original datasets), while MR-Part obtains values for transferred data below 10% for all the queries. Notice that, even with reduce locality-aware scheduling, no gain is obtained in data locality as keys are distributed in all input chunks.

Transferred Data for Different Cluster Sizes. In the next scenario, we have chosen query Q5, and measured the transferred data in the shuffle phase by varying the cluster size and input data size. Input data size has been scaled

---

[3] We have used the implementation provided in
http://www.cs.duke.edu/starfish/mr-apps.html

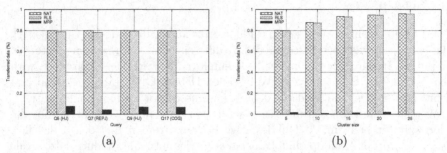

Fig. 2. Percentage of transferred data for a) different type of queries b) varying cluster and data size

depending on the cluster size, so that each node is assigned 2GB of data. Fig 2(b) shows the percentage of transferred data for the three approaches, while increasing the number of cluster nodes. As shown, with increasing the number of nodes, our approach maintains a steady data locality, but it decreases for the other approaches. Since there is no skew in key frequencies, both native Hadoop and RLS obtain data localities near 1 divided by the number of nodes. Our experiments with different data sizes for the same cluster size show no modification in the percentage of transferred data for MR-Part (the results are not shown in the paper due to space restrictions).

Response Time. As shown in previous subsection, MR-Part can significantly reduce the amount of transferred data in the shuffle phase. However, its impact on response time strongly depends on the network bandwidth. In this section, we measure the effect of MR-Part on MapReduce response time by varying network bandwidth. We control point-to-point bandwidth by using Linux `tc` command line utility. We execute query Q5 on a cluster of 20 nodes with scale factor of 40 (40GB of dataset total size).

The results are shown in Fig 3. As we can see in Fig 3 (a), the slower is the network, the biggest is the impact of data locality on execution time. To show where the improvement is produced, in Fig 3 (b) we report the time spent in data shuffling. Measuring shuffle time is not straightforward since in native Hadoop it starts once 5% of map tasks have finished and proceeds in parallel while they are completed. Because of that, we represent two lines: NAT-ms that represents the time spent since the first shuffle byte is sent until this phase is completed, and NAT-os that represents the period of time where the system is only dedicated to shuffling (after last map finishes). For MR-Part only the second line has to be represented as the system has to wait for all map tasks to complete in order to schedule reduce tasks. We can observe that, while shuffle time is almost constant for MR-Part, regardless of the network conditions, it increases significantly as the network bandwidth decreases for the other alternatives. As a consequence, the response time for MR-Part is less sensitive to the network bandwidth than that of native Hadoop. For instance, for 10mbps, MR-Part executes in around 30% less time than native Hadoop.

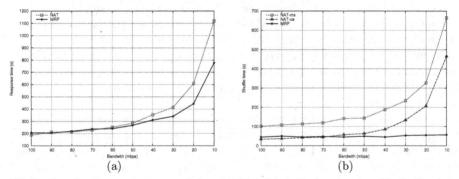

Fig. 3. Results for varying network bandwidth: a) total response time b) shuffle time

5   Related Work

Reducing data transfer in the shuffle phase is important because it may impose a significant overhead in job execution. In [12] a simulation is carried out in order to study the performance of MapReduce in different scenarios. The results show that data shuffling may take an important part of the job execution, particularly when network links are shared among different nodes belonging to a rack or a network topology. In [11], a pre-shuffling scheme is proposed to reduce data transfers in the shuffle phase. It looks over the input splits before the map phase begins and predicts the reducer the key-value pairs are partitioned into. Then, the data is assigned to a map task near the expected future reducer. Similarly, in [5], reduce tasks are assigned to the nodes that reduce the network transfers among nodes and racks. However, in this case, the decision is taken at reduce scheduling time. In [10] a set of data and VM placement techniques are proposed to improve data locality in shared cloud environments. They classify MapReduce jobs into three classes and use different placement techniques to reduce network transfers. All the mentioned jobs are limited by how the MapReduce partitioning function assigns intermediate keys to reduce tasks. In [7] this problem is addressed by assigning intermediate keys to reducers at scheduling time. However, data locality is limited by how intermediate keys are spread over all the map outputs. MR-part employs this technique as part of the reduce scheduling, but improves its efficiency by partitioning intelligently input data.

Graph and hypergraph partitioning have been used to guide data partitioning in databases and in general in parallel computing [6]. They allow to capture data relationships when no other information, e.g., the schema, is given. The work in [3,8] uses this approach to generate a database partitioning. [3] is similar to our approach in the sense that it tries to co-locate frequently accessed data items, although it is used to avoid distributed transactions in an OLTP system.

6   Conclusions and Future Work

In this paper we proposed MR-Part, a new technique for reducing the transferred data in the MapReduce shuffle phase. MR-Part monitors a set of MapReduce jobs constituting a workload sample and creates a workload model by means of a hypergraph. Then, using the workload model, MR-Part repartitions the input files with the objective of maximizing the data locality in the reduce phase. We have built the prototype of MR-Part in Hadoop, and tested it in Grid5000 experimental platform. Results show a significant reduction in transferred data in the shuffle phase and important improvements in response time when network bandwidth is limited.

As a possible future work we envision to perform the repartitioning in parallel. The approach used in this paper has worked flawlessly for the employed datasets, but a parallel version would be able to scale to very big inputs. This version would need to use parallel graph partitioning libraries, such as Zoltan.

Acknowledgments. Experiments presented in this paper were carried out using the Grid'5000 experimental testbed, being developed under the INRIA ALADDIN development action with support from CNRS, RENATER and several universities as well as other funding bodies (see https://www.grid5000.fr).

References

1. Grid 5000 project, `https://www.grid5000.fr/mediawiki/index.php`
2. Hadoop, `http://hadoop.apache.org`
3. Curino, C., Jones, E., Zhang, Y., Madden, S.: Schism: a workload-driven approach to database replication and partitioning. Proceedings of the VLDB Endowment 3(1), 48–57 (2010)
4. Dean, J., Ghemawat, S.: MapReduce: Simplified data processing on large clusters. In: OSDI, pp. 137–150. USENIX Association (2004)
5. Hammoud, M., Rehman, M.S., Sakr, M.F.: Center-of-gravity reduce task scheduling to lower mapreduce network traffic. In: IEEE CLOUD, pp. 49–58. IEEE (2012)
6. Hendrickson, B., Kolda, T.G.: Graph partitioning models for parallel computing. Parallel Computing 26(12), 1519–1534 (2000)
7. Ibrahim, S., Jin, H., Lu, L., Wu, S., He, B., Qi, L.: LEEN: Locality/fairness-aware key partitioning for mapreduce in the cloud. In: Proceedings of Second International Conference on Cloud Computing, CloudCom 2010, Indianapolis, Indiana, USA, November 30 - December 3, pp. 17–24 (2010)
8. Liu, D.R., Shekhar, S.: Partitioning similarity graphs: a framework for declustering problems. Information Systems 21(6), 475–496 (1996)
9. Olston, C., Reed, B., Srivastava, U., Kumar, R., Tomkins, A.: Pig latin: a not-so-foreign language for data processing. In: SIGMOD Conference, pp. 1099–1110. ACM (2008)
10. Palanisamy, B., Singh, A., Liu, L., Jain, B.: Purlieus: locality-aware resource allocation for mapreduce in a cloud. In: Conference on High Performance Computing Networking, Storage and Analysis, SC 2011, Seattle, WA, USA, November 12-18, p. 58 (2011)
11. Seo, S., Jang, I., Woo, K., Kim, I., Kim, J.S., Maeng, S.: HPMR: Prefetching and pre-shuffling in shared mapreduce computation environment. In: CLUSTER, pp. 1–8. IEEE (2009)
12. Wang, G., Butt, A.R., Pandey, P., Gupta, K.: A simulation approach to evaluating design decisions in mapreduce setups. In: MASCOTS, pp. 1–11. IEEE (2009)

Incremental Algorithms for Selecting Horizontal Schemas of Data Warehouses: The Dynamic Case

Ladjel Bellatreche[1], Rima Bouchakri[2],
Alfredo Cuzzocrea[3], and Sofian Maabout[4]

[1] LIAS/ISAE-ENSMA, Poitiers University, Poitiers, France
[2] National High School for Computer Science, Algiers, Algeria
[3] ICAR-CNR and University of Calabria, I-87036 Cosenza, Italy
[4] LABRI, Bordeaux, France
{bellatreche,rima.bouchakri}@ensma.fr,
cuzzocrea@si.deis.unical.it, maabout@labri.fr

Abstract. Looking at the problem of *effectively and efficiently partitioning data warehouses*, most of state-of-the-art approaches, which are very often *heuristic-based*, are static, since they assume the existence of an a-priori known set of queries. Contrary to this, in real-life applications, queries may change dynamically and fragmentation heuristics need to integrate these changes. Following this main consideration, in this paper we propose and experimentally assess *an incremental approach for selecting data warehouse fragmentation schemes using genetic algorithms*.

1 Introduction

In decisional applications, important data are imbedded, historized, and stored in relational Data Warehouses (DW) that are often modeled using a star schema or one of its variations [15] to perform an online analytical processing. The queries that are executed on the DW are called *star join queries*, because they contain several complex joins and selection operations that involve fact tables and several dimension tables. In order to optimize such complex operations, optimization techniques, like Horizontal Data Partitioning (HDP), need to be implemented during the *physical design*. The horizontal data partitioning consists in segmenting a table, an index or a materialized view, into *horizontal partitions* [20]. Initially, horizontal data partitioning is proposed as a logical design technique of relational and object databases [13]. Currently, it's used in physical design of data warehouse. Horizontal data partitioning has two important characteristics: (1) it is considered as a non-redundant optimization structure because it doesn't require additional space storage [16] and (2) it is applied during the creation of the data warehouse. Two types of horizontal data partitioning exist and supported by commercial DBMS: *mono table partitioning* and *table-dependent partitioning* [18]. In the mono table partitioning, a table is partitioned using its own attributes. Several modes are proposed to implement this partitioning:

A. Hameurlain, W. Rahayu, and D. Taniar (Eds.): Globe 2013, LNCS 8059, pp. 13–25, 2013.

Range, List, Hash, Composite (*List-List, Range-List, Range-Range*, etc.). Mono table partitioning is used to optimize selections operations, when partitioning key represents their attributes. In table-dependent partitioning, a table inherits the partitioning characteristics from other table. In a data warehouse modeled using a star schema, the fact table may be partitioned based on the fragmentation schemas of dimension tables due to the *parent-child relationship* that exist among the fact table, which optimizes selections and joins simultaneously. Note that a fragmentation schemas results of partitioning process of dimension tables. This partitioning is supported by Oracle11G under the name *referential partitioning*.

The horizontal data partitioning got a lot of attention from academic and industrial communities. Most works, that propose a fragmentation schema selection, can be classified into two main categories according to the selection algorithm: *Affinity and COM-MIN based algorithms* and *Cost based algorithms*. In the first ones (e.g., [4, 21, 17]) a cost model and a control on the number of generated fragments are used in fragmentation schema selection. In the second ones (e.g., [2, 4, 9], the fragmentation schema is evaluated using a *cost model* in order to estimate the reduction of queries complexity.

When analyzing these works, we conclude that the horizontal data partitioning selection problem consists in selecting a fragmentation schema that optimizes a *static set of queries* (all the queries are known in advance) under a given constraint (e.g., [5, 6]). These approach do not deal with the workload evolution. In fact, if a given attribute is not often used to interrogate the data warehouse, why keeping a fragmentation schema on this attribute, especially when a constraint on the fragments number of fact table is defined. It would be better to merge the fragments defined on this attribute and split the data warehouse fragments according to another attribute most frequently used by queries. So, we present in this article an *incremental approach for selecting horizontal data partitioning schema in data warehouse using genetic algorithms*. It's based on adapting the current fragmentation schema of the data warehouse in order to deal with the workload evolutions.

The proposed approach is oriented to cover optimal fragmentation schemes of very large relational data warehouses. Given this, it can be easily used in the context of both *Grid* (e.g., [10–12]) and *P2P* (e.g., [7]) computing environments. A preliminary, shorter version of this paper appears in [3]. With respect to [3], in this paper we provide more theoretical and practical contributions of the proposed framework along with its experimental assessment.

This article is organized as follows: Section 2 reviews the horizontal data partitioning selection problem. Section 3 describes the static selection of a fragmentation schema using genetic algorithms. Section 4 describes our incremental horizontal data partitioning selection. Section 5 experimentally shows the benefits coming from our proposal. Section 6 concludes the paper.

2 Horizontal Data Partitioning Selection Problem in Data Warehouses

In order to optimize relational OLAP queries, that involve restrictions and joins, using HDP, authors in [4] show that the best partitioning scenario of a relational data warehouse is performed as follow : a mono table partitioning of the dimension tables is performed, followed by a table-dependent partitioning of the fact table according to fragmentation schema of dimension tables. The problem of HDP is formalized in the context of relational data warehouses as follows [4, 9, 19]:

Given (i) a representative workload $\mathcal{Q} = \{Q_1, ..., Q_n\}$, where each query Q_i ($1 \leq i \leq n$) has an access frequency f_i, defined on a relational data warehouse schema with d dimension tables $\{D_1, ..., D_d\}$ and a fact table F from which a set of fragmentation attribute[1] $AS = \{A_1, \cdots , A_n\}$ are extracted and (ii) a constraint (called maintenance bound B given by Administrator) representing the maximum number of fact fragments that he/she wants.

The problem of HDP consists in identifying the fragmentation schema FS of dimension table(s) that could be used to referential partition the fact table F into N fragments, such that the queries cost is minimized and the maintenance constraint is satisfied ($N \leq B$). This problem is an NP-hard [4]. Several types of algorithms to find a near-optimal solution are proposed: genetic, simulated annealing, greedy, data mining driven algorithms [4, 9]. In Section 3, we present the static selection of fragmentation schema based on work in [4].

3 Static Selection of Data Warehouse Fragmentation Schemas Using Genetic Algorithms

We present in this Section a static approach for selecting fragmentation schemas on a set of fragmentation attributes, using Genetic Algorithms (GA). The GA is an iterative search algorithm of optimum based on the process of natural evolution. It manipulates a population of chromosomes that encode solutions of the selection problems (in our case a solution is a fragmentation schema). Each chromosome contains a set of genes where each gene takes values from a specific alphabet [1]. In each GA iteration, a new population is created based on the last population by applying genetics operations such as mutation, selection, and crossover, using a fitness function which evaluate the benefit of the current chromosomes (solutions). The main difficulty in using the GA is to define the chromosome encoding that must represent a fragmentation schema. In a fragmentation schema, each horizontal fragment is specified by a set of predicates that are defined on fragmentation attributes, where each attribute has a domain of values. Using these predicates, each attribute domain can be divided into sub domains. For example, given a dimension table $Customers$ with and attribute $City$, a domain of $City$ is $Dom(City)=\{$ 'Algiers', 'Paris'$\}$. This means that the

---

[1] A fragmentation attribute appears in selection predicates of the WHERE clause.

predicates *"City='Algiers'"* and *"City='Paris'"* defines two horizontal fragments of dimension *Customers*. So, a fragmentation schema can be specified by an attributes domain partitioning. The attributes domain partitioning is represented by an array of vectors where each vector characterizes an attribute and each cell of the vector refers to a sub domain of the corresponding attribute. A cell contains a number so that the sub domains with the same number are merged into one sub domain. This array is the encoding of the chromosome.

In order to select the better fragmentation schema by GA, we use a mathematical cost model to define the fitness function [4]. The cost model estimates the number of inputs outputs (I/O in terms of pages) required to execute the queries on a partitioned DW. We consider a DW with a fact table F and d dimension tables $D = \{D_1, D_2, ..., D_d\}$. The horizontal partitioning of DW according to a given fragmentation schema $\mathcal{SF}$ generates N sub star schemas $\mathcal{SF} = \{S_1, ..., S_N\}$. Let a workload of t queries $Q = \{Q_1, Q_2, ..., Q_t\}$. The cost of executing Q_k on $\mathcal{SF}$ is the sum of the execution cost of Q_k on each sub star schemas S_i. In S_i a fact fragment is specified by M_i predicates $\{PF_1, ..., PF_{M_i}\}$ and a dimension fragment D_s is specified by L_s predicates $\{PM_1^s, ..., PM_{L_s}^s\}$. The loading cost of a fact fragment is $\prod_{j=1}^{M_i} Sel(PF_j) \times |F|$ and for dimension fragment D_s is : $\prod_{j=1}^{L_s} Sel(PM_j^s) \times |D_s|$, where $|R|$ and $Sel(P)$ represent the pages number occupied by R and the selectivity of the predicate P. The execution cost of Q_k on S_i computes the loading cost of fact fragment and the hash join with the dimension fragment as follow: $Cost(Q_k, S_i) = [3 \times [\prod_{j=1}^{M_i} Sel(PF_j) \times |F| + \sum_{k=1}^{d} \prod_{j=1}^{L_s} Sel(PM_j^s) \times |D_s|]]$. In order to estimate Q_k execution cost on the partitioned DW, the valid sub schemas of the query must be identified. A valid sub schema is acceded by the query on at least one fact instance. Let NS_k be the number of Q_k valid sub schemas. The total execution cost of Q_k on the DW is $Cost(Q_k, \mathcal{SF}) = \sum_{j=1}^{NS_k} Cost(Q_k, S_j)$, and the total execution cost of the workload is given by :

$$Cost(Q, SF) = \sum_{k=1}^{t} Cost(Q_k, SF) \tag{1}$$

Once the cost model presented, the fitness function can be introduced. The GA manipulates a chromosomes population in each iteration (fragmentations schemas). Let m be the population size $SF_1, ..., SF_m$. Given a constraint on the maximum fragments number B, the genetic algorithm can generate solutions SF_i with a fragments number that exceeds B. Therefore, these fragmentation schemas should be penalized. The penalty function of a schema is: $Pen(SF_i) = \frac{N_i}{B}$, where N_i is the number of sub schemas of SF_i. Finally, the GA selects a fragmentation schema that minimizes the following fitness function:

$$F(SF_i) = \begin{cases} Cost(Q,SF_i) \times Pen(SF_i), if Pen(SF_i) > 1 \\ Cost(Q,SF_i), otherwise \end{cases} \tag{2}$$

Once the chromosome encoding and fitness function computing are defined, the GA selection can be performed following these three steps: (1) Code the fragmentation schemas into a chromosomes. (2) Define the fitness function. (3) Select optimal fragmentation schema by Genetic Algorithms : To realize the GA selection, we use a JAVA API called $JGAP^2$ (Java Genetic Algorithms Package) that implements genetic algorithms. JGAP needs two inputs: the chromosome encoding and the fitness function, it gives in output the optimal (near-optimal) fragmentation schema. The JGAP API is based on a GA process : GA generate an initial population of chromosomes, then performs genetic operations (selection, mutation, crossover) in order to generate new populations. Each chromosome is evaluated by fitness function in order to estimate the benefit given by the fragmentation schema to the workload performance. The process of HDP selection by GA is given as follow:

HDP **selection by** GA
Input:

Q : workload of t queries
AS : n fragmentation attributes $AS = \{A_1, \cdots, A_n\}$
Dom : attributes domains $Dom = \{Dom_1, \cdots, Dom_n\}$
DW : Data of the cost model (table size, system page etc.)
B : maintenance bound given by Administrator (maximum number of fact fragments)

Output: fragmentation schema SF.
Notations:

$Chrom\_Encoding$: Encode a fragmentation schema into a chromosome
$FitnessHDP$: fitness function for the GA
$JGAP$: JAVA API that implements the GA

Begin

$ChromosomeHDP = Chrom\_Encoding(AS, Dom);$
$FitnessHDP = Genetic\_FitnessFonction(Q, AS, B, DW);$
$SF = JGAP(ChromosomeHDP, FitnessHDP);$

End

4   Incremental Selection of Data Warehouse Fragmentation Schemas Using Genetic Algorithms

In the context of physical design of data warehouse, many studies are focused on HDP selection problem in order to define fragmentation schema that improves a workload performance. But the majority of these works define a static approach that can't deal with changes occurring on DW, specially the execution of news queries that not exist in the current workload. To achieve incremental selection of a fragmentation schema, we must adjust the current fragmentation schema of DW by taking into account the execution of a new query Q_i. Running Q_i

---
[2] http://jgap.sourceforge.net

may cause the addition of new fragmentation attributes or the extension of attributes domains. This will cause merge and split operations on *DW* fragments. Under the Oracle DBMS, it is possible to adapt a partitioned *DW* according to a new fragmentation schema using the operations SPLIT PARTITION and MERGE PARTITION. The operation MERGE PARTITION combines two fragments into one, thus reducing the number of fragments. In the other hand, the SPLIT PARTITION operation divides a fragment to create new fragments. This increases the number of total fragments.

Example. We consider a *DW* containing a fact table Sales and a dimension table Customers partitioned according to the schema given by Figure 1.a. The partitioned table Customers is given by Figure 1.b.

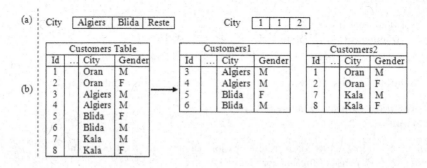

Fig. 1. (a) Fragmentation schema. (b) Partitioned dimension Customers.

Suppose the execution of the following new query :

```
SELECT AVG(Prix)
FROM Sales S, Customers C
WHERE S.IdC=C.IdC AND C.Gender = 'F'
```

In order to take into account the optimization of this new query, a new fragmentation schema is selected (Figure 2.a). Adapting this new schema on the *DW* requires two SPLIT operations on Customers, the result is given by Figure 2.b

The main challenge of the incremental approach is defining a selection process that takes into account workload evolution. First, we propose a Naive Incremental Selection (*NIS*) based on merge and split operations. Subsequently, we adapt the static approach for selecting fragmentation schemas defined in Section 3, and we introduce two incremental approaches based on genetic algorithms (*ISGA* and *ISGA**).

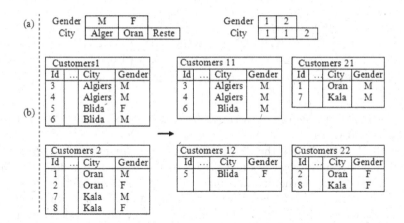

Fig. 2. (a) New fragmentation schema. (b) Update of the dimension Customers fragmentation.

4.1   Naive Incremental Selection (*NIS*)

Consider a *DW* on which a set of queries are executed successively. The Naive Incremental Selection *NIS* starts from an initial fragmentation schema, that optimizes the current workload. On the execution of a new query Q_i, the chromosome is updated according to the attributes and values contained in Q_i. If the constraint B (maximum number of fact fragments) is violated, a Merge operation is performed to reduce the number of generated fragments. The Merge operation consists in merging two sub domains of a given attribute in a single sub domain. Let consider a *Customers* table partitioned into three fragments on the attribute *City*: *Client1*: (*City* = 'Algiers'), *Client2*: (*City* = 'Oran') and *Client3*: (*City* = Blida). If the two sub domains *Oran* and *Blida* are merged, the *Customers* table will be partitioned into two fragments *Client1*: (*City* = 'Algiers') and *Client2*: (*City* = 'Oran' or 'Blida'). To realize the naive incremental selection using genetic algorithms, we adapt the static selection of fragmentation schema defined in Section 3. We use the chromosome encoding to represent a fragmentation schema, then when running a new query Q_i, we realize the naive selection by executing the following operations on the chromosome Ch :

1. Extract from Q_i fragmentation attributes A_j and their corresponding values V_{jk} that appear in the selection predicates. A selection predicate P is represented as follow : " Aj op V_{jk} ", where *op* in $\{=, <, >, <>, \leq, \geq\}$. We consider the fragmentation schema given in the Figure 2.a. Suppose the execution of the following query:

```
SELECT AVG(Prix)
FROM Sales S, Customers C, ProdTable P
WHERE S.IdC=C.IdC AND S.IdP=P.IdP
AND P.Product = 'P4'
AND (C.City = 'Algiers' OR C.City = 'Oran')
```

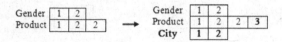

Fig. 3. NIS : update the encoding of chromosome Ch

We extract from the query the attributes Product, City and the values P4, Algiers and Oran.

2. Update the encoding of the chromosome Ch according to the attributes and their sub domains obtained in (1). We assign to each sub domain a new value. According to the previous query, Ch update is given in Figure 3

3. If the constraint B is violated (the fragments number $> B$) : (a) Order the attributes according to their frequency of use by the workload, from the least used to the most used. (b) For each attribute, order the sub domains according to their frequency of use by the workload, from the least used to the most used. (c) Merge attributes sub domains until obtaining a fragmentation schema that doesn't violate the constraint B. Let consider the order, *City, Product, Gender*, and a constraint $B = 4$, the merges operations on the chromosome Ch are given in Figure 4. The fragmentation schema has four resulting fragments, 2 on *Product* and 2 on *Gender*.

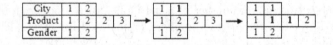

Fig. 4. NIS : successive merging applied on chromosome Ch

4.2   Incremental Selection Based on Genetic Algorithms ($ISGA$)

We adapt the static approach based on genetic algorithm presented above. Upon execution of each query, the encoding of the chromosome is updated by taking into account the changes given by the query. Consider the fragmentation schema given in Figure 5.

Suppose the execution of the following new query:

```
SELECT AVG(Prix)
FROM Sales S, Customers C, ProdTable P
WHERE S.IdC=C.IdC AND S.IdP=P.IdP AND
(C.Pays = 'Algeria' or C.Pays = 'Tunisia')
AND P.Product = 'P4'
```

The chromosome encoding update is given in the Figure 6.

After updating the chromosome encoding, the selection of a fragmentation schema based on GA is performed. The main problem with this approach is that the selection process does not take into account the current fragmentation

Gender	M	F		
Product	P1	P2	P3	Reste
City	Algiers	Oran	Blida	Kala	Reste

Gender	1	2		
Product	1	2	2	2
City	1	2	3	3	3

Fig. 5. $ISGA$: an example of a chromosome

Gender	M	F		
Product	P1	P2	P3	P4	Reste
City	Algiers	Oran	Blida	Kala	Reste
Country	Algeria	Tunisia	Reste	

Gender	1	2		
Product	1	2	2	3	2
City	1	2	3	3	3
Country	1	2	3	

Fig. 6. $ISGA$: update the chromosome encoding

schema of the data warehouse. Indeed, to adapt a new fragmentation schema on a DW already fragmented, merges and/or splits operations are required. Therefore, a new fragmentation schema can significantly improve query execution performance but can require a high maintenance cost. Thus, we propose a new incremental selection approach based on genetic algorithms that we introduce in Section 4.3.

4.3   Improved Incremental Selection Based on Genetic Algorithms ($ISGA^*$)

In order to reduce the maintenance cost of a new fragmentation schema, we propose to improve our $ISGA$ approach. The main idea of this new approach is to change the fitness function, that evaluates the various solutions generated by GA, and penalize solutions representing fragmentation schemas with a high cost of maintenance. The cost of maintenance represents the number of merges and splits operations required to implement the new fragmentation schema on a partitioned DW. In order to evaluate the cost of maintenance, we define a function called Function of Dissimilarity FD whose signature is given as follows:

$FD(SF_i)$ = number of merge and split operations needed to update the partitioned DW according to a given fragmentation schema SF_i (chromosome). In Figure 7, we present two fragmentation schemas, the actual fragmentation schema of the data warehouse and a new schema being evaluated by the genetic algorithm. For the example illustrated in Figure 7, $FD(SF_i) = 1$ Split on

Current fragmentation schema

Gender	1	2		
Product	1	1	2	2	2
City	1	2	3	3	3
Country	1	2	3	

New fragmentation schema SF_i

Gender	1	2		
Product	1	1	2	3	2
City	1	2	2	3	3
Country	1	1	2	

Fig. 7. $ISGA^*$ selection: real vs. new fragmentation schema of DW

Product + 1 Split on *City* + 1 Merge on *City* + 1 Merge on *Country* = 4. Recall that the fitness function of the genetic algorithm is given as follows:

$$F(SF_i) = \{ {Cost(Q,SF_i) \times Pen(SF_i), if Pen(SF_i) > 1 \atop Cost(Q,SF_i), otherwise} \tag{3}$$

where $Pen(SF_i) = N_i/B$. We propose to define a new penalty function $Pen2(SF_i) = FD(SF_i)$. So the new fitness function is given by : $F'(SF_i) = F(SF_i) \times FD(SF_i)$.

5   Experimental Assessment and Analysis

In order to compare different strategies of incremental selection of HDP, we conduct several comparison tests on a real data warehouse from the APB1 benchmark [8]. we create and populate the data warehouse with a star schema containing a fact table *Actvars* (24 786 000 tuples) and 4 dimension tables *Prodlevel* (9000 tuples), *Custlevel* (900 tuples), *Timelevel* (24 tuples) and *Chanlevel* (9 tuples). The GA is implemented using the JAVA API $JGAP$. Our tests are performed in two phases: we conduct small-scale tests on a workload of 8 queries, then we realize large-scale tests on a workload of 60 queries. Note that the 60 queries generate *18 indexable attributes (Line, Day, Week, Country, Depart, Type, Sort, Class, Group, Family, Division, Year, Month, Quarter, Retailer, City, Gender and All)* that respectively have the following cardinalities : 15, 31, 52, 11, 25, 25, 4, 605, 300, 75, 4, 2, 12, 4, 99, 4, 2, 3

5.1   Small-Scale Tests

In this experiment, we first consider an empty workload. Then, we suppose that eight new queries are successively executed on the DW. Each new query triggers an incremental selection, under a constraint $B = 40$. We run the three approaches (NIS, $ISGA$, $ISGA^*$) and for each selection and each new query, we note two information : (1) the cost optimization rate of the executed queries (Figure 8 (a))

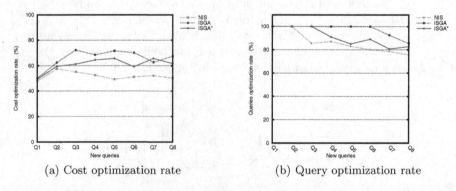

(a) Cost optimization rate   (b) Query optimization rate

Fig. 8. Performance analysis when considering a query workload having 8 queries

and (2) the queries optimization rate (Figure 8 (*b*)). We note that the best results are given by the approach $ISGA^*$. Indeed, the execution cost is reduced by 70%, for 95% queries optimized. By cons, $ISGA^*$ gives fragmentation schemas which require several mergers and splits for the implementation on DW. To better see the effectiveness of our incremental strategy and for a better comparison, we conducted large-scale testing.

5.2 Large-Scale Tests

We consider a workload of 40 queries executed on a partitioned DW. The current fragmentation schema of the DW is obtained by a static selection using the 40 queries with a constraint $B = 100$. After that, we suppose that 20 new queries are successively executed on the DW. Each new query triggers an incremental selection, under a constraint $B = 100$. We run the three approaches (NIS, $ISGA$, $ISGA^*$) and for each approach and each new query, we note the cost optimization rate of the executed queries (Figure 9 (*a*)).

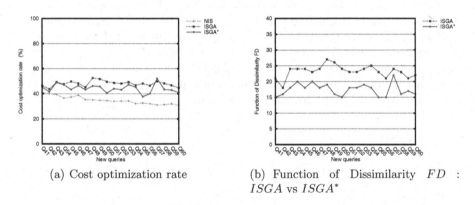

(a) Cost optimization rate

(b) Function of Dissimilarity FD : $ISGA$ vs $ISGA^*$

Fig. 9. Performance analysis when considering a query workload having 20 queries

This experiment shows that using genetic algorithms in incremental approaches ($ISGA$ and $ISGA^*$) gives better optimization than the naive incremental approach. Indeed, $ISGA$ provides an average reduction of 45% of the queries cost and $ISGA^*$ gives an improvement of 42% against 37% for NIS. Comparing the two approaches $ISGA$ and $ISGA^*$, we notice that $ISGA$ gives better results. Indeed, in the approach $ISGA^*$, solutions that are dissimilar to the current fragmentation schema of the DW are penalized (schemas that requires several mergers and splits operations). Thus, in $ISGA^*$ good solutions, which improve query performance, may be excluded by the selection process. However, in the $ISGA$ approach, the genetic algorithm selects a final solution with a high maintenance cost. To illustrate this problem, we noted during the previous test the value of the function of dissimilarity FD of each final fragmentation schema selected by the two approaches $ISGA$ and $ISGA^*$. The result is shown in Figure9 (*b*). This figure clearly shows that the final solutions selected by $ISGA^*$ require more merges and splits operations than the solutions selected by $ISGA$. Thus, according to the two important parameters namely: the optimization of the workload cost and the maintenance cost of a selected schema, the approach $ISGA^*$ is a better proposal than both $ISGA$ and NIS approaches.

6   Conclusions and Future Work

We proposed an incremental approach based on genetic algorithms that deals with workload evolutions, unlike the static approach. In order to perform the incremental selection using genetic algorithms, we propose a standard chromosome encoding that define a fragmentation schema. Three strategies were proposed: (1) the naive incremental approach NIS that uses simple operations to adapt the DW fragmentation schema according to the workload changes, (2) incremental approach of a new fragmentation schema based on genetic algorithm $ISGA$, and (3) improved incremental approach based on genetic algorithm, $ISGA^*$, which overcomes $ISGA$ approach because the latter penalizes high maintenance cost solutions. We also conducted an experimental study. The results show that the $ISGA^*$ approach is a good compromise between the naive approach and the approach by genetic algorithm. It gives a better optimization of queries while reducing the maintenance cost. Future work considers other changes that may occur on the data warehouse, beyond to workload changes, such as: changing the queries access frequency [14], changes on the population of the data warehouse, modifications on the data warehouse schema, and so forth.

References

1. Bäck, T.: Evolutionnary algorithms in theory and practice. Oxford University Press, New York (1995)
2. Bellatreche, L.: Dimension table selection strategies to referential partition a fact table of relational data warehouses. In: Recent Trends in Information Reuse and Integration, pp. 19–42. Springer (2012)
3. Bellatreche, L., Bouchakri, R., Cuzzocrea, A., Maabout, S.: Horizontal partitioning of very-large data warehouses under dynamically-changing query workloads via incremental algorithms. In: SAC, pp. 208–210 (2013)
4. Bellatreche, L., Boukhalfa, K., Richard, P.: Referential horizontal partitioning selection problem in data warehouses: Hardness study and selection algorithms. International Journal of Data Warehousing and Mining 5(4), 1–23 (2009)
5. Bellatreche, L., Cuzzocrea, A., Benkrid, S.: F&a: A methodology for effectively and efficiently designing parallel relational data warehouses on heterogenous database clusters. In: DaWak, pp. 89–104 (2010)
6. Bellatreche, L., Cuzzocrea, A., Benkrid, S.: Effectively and efficiently designing and querying parallel relational data warehouses on heterogeneous database clusters: The f&a approach 23(4), 17–51 (2012)
7. Bonifati, A., Cuzzocrea, A.: Efficient fragmentation of large XML documents. In: Wagner, R., Revell, N., Pernul, G. (eds.) DEXA 2007. LNCS, vol. 4653, pp. 539–550. Springer, Heidelberg (2007)

8. OLAP Council. Apb-1 olap benchmark, release ii (1998), http://www.olapcouncil.org/research/bmarkly.htm

9. Cuzzocrea, A., Darmont, J., Mahboubi, H.: Fragmenting very large xml data warehouses via k-means clustering algorithm. IJBIDM 4(3/4), 301–328 (2009)

10. Cuzzocrea, A., Furfaro, F., Greco, S., Masciari, E., Mazzeo, G.M., Saccà, D.: A distributed system for answering range queries on sensor network data. In: PerCom Workshops, pp. 369–373 (2005)

11. Cuzzocrea, A., Furfaro, F., Mazzeo, G.M., Saccá, D.: A grid framework for approximate aggregate query answering on summarized sensor network readings. In: Meersman, R., Tari, Z., Corsaro, A. (eds.) OTM-WS 2004. LNCS, vol. 3292, pp. 144–153. Springer, Heidelberg (2004)

12. Cuzzocrea, A., Saccà, D.: Exploiting compression and approximation paradigms for effective and efficient online analytical processing over sensor network readings in data grid environments. In: Concurrency and Computation: Practice and Experience (2013)

13. Karlapalem, K., Li, Q.: A framework for class partitioning in object-oriented databases. Distributed and Parallel Databases 8(3), 333–366 (2000)

14. Karlapalem, K., Navathe, S.B., Ammar, M.H.: Optimal redesign policies to support dynamic processing of applications on a distributed relational database system. Information Systems 21(4), 353–367 (1996)

15. Kimball, R., Strehlo, K.: Why decision support fails and how to fix it. SIGMOD Record 24(3), 92–97 (1995)

16. Bellatreche, L., Boukhalfa, K., Mohania, M.K.: Pruning search space of physical database design. In: Wagner, R., Revell, N., Pernul, G. (eds.) DEXA 2007. LNCS, vol. 4653, pp. 479–488. Springer, Heidelberg (2007)

17. Özsu, M.T., Valduriez, P.: Distributed database systems: Where are we now? IEEE Computer 24(8), 68–78 (1991)

18. Özsu, M.T., Valduriez, P.: Principles of Distributed Database Systems, 2nd edn. Prentice Hall (1999)

19. Papadomanolakis, S., Ailamaki, A.: Autopart: Automating schema design for large scientific databases using data partitioning. In: Proceedings of the 16th International Conference on Scientific and Statistical Database Management (SSDBM 2004), pp. 383–392 (June 2004)

20. Sanjay, A., Narasayya, V.R., Yang, B.: Integrating vertical and horizontal partitioning into automated physical database design. In: Proceedings of the ACM SIGMOD International Conference on Management of Data, pp. 359–370 (June 2004)

21. Zhang, Y., Orlowska, M.-E.: On fragmentation for distributed database design. Information Sciences 1(3), 117–132 (1994)

Scalable and Fully Consistent Transactions in the Cloud through Hierarchical Validation*

Jon Grov[1,2] and Peter Csaba Ölveczky[1,3]

[1] University of Oslo
[2] Bekk Consulting AS
[3] University of Illinois at Urbana-Champaign

Abstract. Cloud-based systems are expected to provide both high availability and low latency regardless of location. For data management, this requires replication. However, transaction management on replicated data poses a number of challenges. One of the most important is isolation: Coordinating simultaneous transactions in a local system is relatively straightforward, but for databases distributed across multiple geographical sites, this requires costly message exchange. Due to the resulting performance impact, available solutions for scalable data management in the cloud work either by reducing consistency standards (e.g., to eventual consistency), or by partitioning the data set and providing consistent execution only within each partition. In both cases, application development is more costly and error-prone, and for critical applications where consistency is crucial, e.g., stock trading, it may seriously limit the possibility to adopt a cloud infrastructure. In this paper, we propose a new method for coordinating transactions on replicated data. We target cloud systems with distribution across a wide-area network. Our approach is based on partitioning data to allow efficient local coordination while providing full consistency through a hierarchical validation procedure across partitions. We also present results from an experimental evaluation using Real-Time Maude simulations.

1 Introduction

Cloud-based systems are expected to provide good performance combined with high availability and ubiquitous access, regardless of physical location and system load. Data management services in the cloud also need database features such as transactions, which allow users to execute groups of operations atomically and consistently. For many applications, including payroll management, banking, resource booking (e.g., tickets), shared calendars, and stock trading, a database providing consistency through transactions is crucial to enable cloud adoption.

To achieve high availability and ubiquitous access, cloud-based databases require data replication. Replication improves availability, since data are accessible even if a server fails, and ubiquitous access, since copies of data can be placed

---

* This work was partially supported by AFOSR Grant FA8750-11-2-0084.

A. Hameurlain, W. Rahayu, and D. Taniar (Eds.): Globe 2013, LNCS 8059, pp. 26–38, 2013.

near the users. Replication may also increase scalability as the workload can be distributed among multiple hosts. Unfortunately, transaction management on replicated data is hard. Managing concurrent access on replicated data requires coordination, and if copies are separated by slow network links, this may increase transaction latency beyond acceptable bounds.

These challenges have made most cloud-based databases relax consistency. Several applications use *data stores*, which abandon transaction support to reduce latency and increase availability. Notable examples of such data stores are Amazon's Dynamo [1], Cassandra [2], and Google BigTable [3]. A recent trend is data stores with transactional capabilities *within* partitions of the data set. Examples include ElaStraS [4], Spinnaker [5] and Google's Megastore [6]. All of these provide high availability, but the transaction support is limited as there is no isolation among transactions accessing different partitions. This imposes strict limits on how to partition the data, and reduce the general applicability.

Managing consistency in applications without transaction support is difficult and expensive [7]. Furthermore, inconsistencies related to concurrent transactions can potentially go undetected for a long time. Google's Spanner [8] combines full consistency with scalability, availability, and low latency in a system replicated across a large geographical area (both sides of the US). However, Spanner is deployed on a complex infrastructure based on GPS and atomic clocks, which limits its applicability as a general-purpose solution.

In this paper, we propose a method for managing replicated data which provides low latency, transaction support, and scalability, *without* requiring specific infrastructure. Our approach, *FLACS* (Flexible, Location-Aware Consistency), is based on the observation that in cloud systems, transactions accessing the same data often originate in the same area. In a world wide online bookstore, the chance is high that most transactions from Spain access Spanish books, while German customers buy German book. For this, partitioning the database according to language would work with traditional methods. However, since we also need to support customers purchasing books both in Spanish and in German, a more sophisticated solution is needed.

FLACS provides full consistency across partitions by organizing the sites in a tree structure, and allow transactions to be validated and committed as near their originating site as possible. To facilitate this, we propose an incremental ordering protocol which allows validation without full view of concurrent transactions. For many usage patterns, this allows the majority of transactions to execute with minimal delay.

We have formally specified the FLACS protocol as a real-time rewrite theory [9], and have used Real-Time Maude [9] simulations to compare the performance of FLACS to a classical approach with a master-site for validation.

The rest of the paper is structured as follows. Section 2 defines our system model. Section 3 gives an overview of the FLACS protocol. Section 4 explains the protocol in more detail. Section 5 presents our simulation results. Finally, Section 6 discusses related work and Section 7 gives some concluding remarks.

2   System Model

We formalize a system for storing and accessing replicated data as a tuple $(P, U, I, O, T, Q, D, lb)$ where:

- P is a finite set (of process identifiers representing a set of real-world *processes*, typically a set of network hosts).
- U is a set (representing possible *data values*).
- I is a set (of identifiers for logical data items).
- $O \subseteq (\{read\} \times I) \cup (\{write\} \times I \times U)$ is a set of possible operations on items.
- T is a set (of transaction identifiers).
- Q is a set of transactions of the form $(t, p, O_{t,p}, <_{t,p})$, where $t \in T$ is the transaction identifier, $p \in P$ is the process hosting transaction, $O_{t,p} \subseteq O$ is the set of operations executed by t on p and $<_{t,p}$ is a partial order on $O_{t,p}$.
- $D \subseteq I \times U \times P$ is a set (with (i, u, p) a replica of i with value u at p).
- lb is a function $lb : P \times P \to \mathbb{N}$ (denoting the lower bound on the message transmission time from p to p').

The *read set* of a transaction $(t, p, O_{t,p}, <_{t,p})$ is the set $RS(t) = \{i \in I \mid (read, i) \in O_{t,p}\}$, and the *write set* of t is $WS(t) = \{i \in I \mid (write, i) \in O_{t,p}\}$. A pair of transactions t, t' are in *conflict* if $WS(t) \cap (RS(t') \cup WS(t')) \neq \emptyset$, or vice versa.

A *read-only transaction* is a transaction t where $WS(t) = \emptyset$. Managing read-only transactions is relatively easy. Therefore, by the term *transaction* we will mean a transaction t with $WS(t) \neq \emptyset$ unless stated otherwise. The treatment of read-only transactions is discussed in Section 3.4.

We assume that processes communicate by message passing, and that each pair (p, p') of processes is connected by a link with minimum message transmission time $lb(p, p')$. We also assume that the underlying infrastructure provides the following operations for inter-process communication:

- *unicast*(m, p, p'), where m is some message, p is the sender and p' is the receiver. Unicast does not guarantee any upper bound on message delivery times nor that messages are delivered in the order in which they were sent.
- *fifoUnicast*(m, p, p'). Similar to unicast, but guarantees that messages between two processes are delivered in the order in which they were sent.

We use simple utility functions for multicast and broadcast built on unicast, and do not assume access to sophisticated group communication middleware.

3   Overview of the FLACS Protocol

State-of-the-art database replication protocols, such as Postgres-R [10] or DBSM [11], provide serializability through optimistic validation combined with *atomic broadcast* to order all transactions before commit. FLACS is an optimistic protocol following a similar approach with one notable exception: FLACS does not require a total order on all transactions before validation. Instead, a transaction t is executed as follows:

1. Execute all operations at the process receiving t (denoted t's initiator).
2. Ordering: A set of processes denoted *observers* are asked to order t against all conflicting transactions. The observers for t are given by $RS(t)$ and $WS(t)$.
3. Validation: Once t is ordered against all conflicting transactions, it is ready for validation. The validating process p is determined by the observers. t is granted commit if and only if for each member i of $RS(t)$, t has read the most recent version of i according to the local order of p.
4. If t is committed, updates are applied according to the order seen by the validator. Otherwise, an abort-message is sent to participating processes.

The purpose of FLACS is to reduce validation delay since coordination among the observers usually requires fewer messages than an atomic broadcast.

3.1   Observers

An observer's task is to serialize updates on its observed items. Formally, an observer function $obs : I \rightarrow \mathcal{P}^+(P)$ maps each item i to its observer(s) $obs(i)$. The idea is to choose as observers processes physically near the most frequent users, and assign items commonly accessed by conflicting transactions to the same observer(s). The observers for a transaction t is the union of the observers for all items in $WS(t)$.

Example 1. Consider a hotel reservation service. Since most reservations are local, *rooms in France* should map to observers physically located in Paris, while *rooms in Germany* are observed by processes in Berlin. As explained below, this allows transactions accessing rooms only in France to commit locally in Paris.

3.2   Ordering

The FLACS validation procedure dictates that a transaction t is granted commit if and only if t has read the most recent version of each $i \in RS(t)$. Since there is no common time among processes, we need to define "most recent." For protocols where transactions are included in a total order before validation, the definition of most recent is simple: it is the most recent according to the total order.

FLACS does not include transactions in a total order before validation. Instead, FLACS uses an incremental ordering and validates a transaction t as soon as it is ordered against all conflicting transactions. Each process p maintains a local, strict partial order $\prec_p$ on the (update) transactions seen so far. Intuitively, $\prec_p$ must order any pair of transactions t, t' known by p to be in conflict. However, the local orders at different processes might be inconsistent. Our idea is to combine these local orders using a tree structure among processes, in which the root of a subtree is responsible for combining the local orders of its descendants, or discovering inconsistencies and resolving them by aborting transactions.

A transaction t can be validated if all observers of items in $WS(t)$ have treated t, and if the local orders of these observers are consistent up to t; i.e., they can be combined into one strict partial order.

The first step of validating a transaction t is to ensure that t is included in the local order of every observer for each item in $WS(t)$. The next step is to merge the local observer orders and check if they are consistent. As explained above, we achieve this by organizing processes in a tree structure, called the *validation hierarchy*. After a transaction is ordered at the observer level, the proposed ordering is propagated upwards in the hierarchy. Eventually, each transaction is included in a total order at the root of the hierarchy; however, the validation (and commit) of a transaction t may take place *before* t is included in this total order, as explained below.

Example 2. Consider the validation hierarchy in Fig. 1. Process p_e represents the European headquarters of our travel agent. Processes p_g and p_f are observers for German and French hotel rooms, respectively. Let t_1 and t_2 be two transactions, reserving one room in Berlin and one room in Paris, respectively, and let t_3 reserve a room in both cities. The orderings then develop as follows:

- p_g orders t_1 and t_3, and all other transactions updating German rooms. The resulting local ordering $\prec_{p_g}$ is then propagated to p_e.
- p_f orders t_2 and t_3, and all other transactions updating French hotel rooms. The resulting local ordering $\prec_{p_f}$ is then propagated to p_e.
- Finally, the local ordering $\prec_{p_e}$ combines $\prec_{p_g}$ and $\prec_{p_f}$

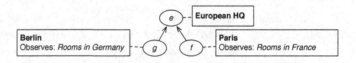

Fig. 1. Example validation hierarchy

Transactions only accessing German rooms can therefore be validated by p_g alone. A transaction accessing *both* German and French rooms is validated by p_e, which combines the orderings of p_g and p_f.

3.3 Validation

We next explain in more detail how a transaction t is validated in FLACS. The validating process p for t, called t's validator, is given as follows:

1. For each item i in $WS(t)$, all observers $obs(i)$ of i are contained in the subtree rooted at p in the validation hierarchy.
2. At least one observer of each item in $RS(t)$ is contained in the subtree rooted at p in the validation hierarchy.
3. No descendant of p in the validation hierarchy satisfies properties 1 and 2.

To validate t, t's initiator sends a validation request to t's validator p containing $RS(t)$, $WS(t)$, $Wval(t)$ (values written by t), and $Rver(t)$ (item versions read by t; each version is represented by the id of the updating transaction). Transaction t is ready for validation once this message is received *and* t is included in $\prec_p$. t

is granted commit if and only if, for each member i of $RS(t)$, $Rver(t)$ contains the most recent version of i according to $\prec_p$.

The correctness argument is the following: To perform this test at the validating process p is equivalent to performing it at the root of the validation hierarchy, where the ordering is global. Since all observers for t are contained within the subtree rooted at p, t's ordering at p is consistent. Additionally, due to the ordering being propagated upwards in the validation hierarchy, we know that any preceding transaction in conflict with t will be known at p upon t's validation. Therefore, the validation test for t at p is equivalent to testing at the root of the validation hierarchy and FLACS guarantees serializability (and consequently, strong consistency).

If t fails the validation test, a message $abort(t)$ is broadcast. Otherwise, a commit message for t is sent to all processes replicating items updated by t. This may include processes that are neither the initiator, observers or part of the validation hierarchy for t. Since transactions updating the same items may be validated by different processes, commit messages can arrive out of order. To handle this, we introduce *sequence numbers*. For an item i, the lowest process p where all $q \in obs(i)$ are in the subtree rooted at p, is responsible for the sequence number of i. Whenever p orders a transaction t updating i, the sequence number of i is incremented and propagated upwards in the validation hierarchy together with the proposed ordering for t. Consequently, t's validator will have a complete set of sequence numbers for items in $WS(t)$. We denote this set $Wseq(t)$.

Upon receiving a commit message $commit(t, WS(t), Wval(t), Wseq(t))$, each process p replicating items in $WS(t)$ initiates a local transaction containing t's write operations. For each item i, the sequence number of the most recent version is stored at p. We refer to this value as $curseq(i,p)$. We then apply Thomas' Write Rule: Let seq_{i_t} represent the sequence number of i created by t. For a replicated item i at process p, we apply t's write operation at p if and only if $curseq(i,p) < seq_{i_t}$.

3.4   Fault Tolerance and Read-Only Transactions

For fault tolerance, our ordering protocol represents the first phase of a two-phase commit. If we assign more than one observer to an item, and then require the validator to synchronize with observers before commit, this item will be accessible as long as a majority of observers are available. In future work, we will combine FLACS with Paxos to provide more sophisticated fault tolerance.

To ensure a consistent read set, a read-only transaction t_r must be executed at, or validated by, a process p_u where, for every item i in $RS(t_r)$, there is at least one observer for i in the subtree rooted by p_u. Read-only transactions requiring "fresh" data follow the same validation procedure as update transactions.

4   The FLACS Protocol

This section presents the FLACS protocol in more detail. The complete formal, executable Real-Time Maude specification of FLACS is available at

http://folk.uio.no/jongr/flacs_model.html. In this paper, we describe the
protocol using pseudocode as a set of *rules*. The following message types are involved in completing the execution of a transaction t:

- *informObserver:* Sent from t's initiator to t's observers to initiate t's ordering.
- *propagateOrder:* Propagate the order upwards in the validation hierarchy.
- *validateRequest:* Sent from t's initiator to its validator (see Section 3.3).
- *commit:* Sent from t's validator to all processes to signal commit.
- *abort:* Sent from a process which determines that t must abort.

The following variables represent the local state of each process p:

- *DATABASE*: A set of records (i, *value*, *seqnum*, *update-history*, *lock-reqs*)
  representing p's version of the database, where *value* is the local value of item
  i; *seqnum* is the sequence number of the most recent update of i; *update-
  history* is a list containing the transaction name of previous updaters of i;
  and *lock-reqs* is a list of requests for either read lock or write lock on i.
- *LOCAL-ORDER*: A list of transaction ids representing the local order at p.
- *REMOTE-TRANS*: The set of currently executing remote transactions.
- *ORDER-GRAPH*: A graph of transactions awaiting to be *ordered* at p.
- *VALIDATE-REQ*: A list representing received validation requests.

```
RULE: EXECUTE-TRANS(t)
while t has more operations do
     (optype,i) = getNextOperation(t)
     wait for lock on i
     when lock granted do executeOperation(t, optype)
     when aborted by high priority transaction do abortTransaction()
ops_t = getExecutedOperations(t)
RS(t) = getReadSet(ops_t)
RVer(t) = findReadVersions(ops_t, DATABASE)
WS(t) = getWriteSet(ops_t)
writeobs = getWriteObservers(WS(t))
validator = findValidator(RS(t), writeobs)
multiCast informObserver(t, WS(t)) from p to writeobs
uniCast validateRequest(t, RS(t), WS(t), WVal(t), RVer(t)) from p to validator
await commit decision
if commit granted then report success to client else report abort to client
releaseLocks(t,DATABASE)
```

Fig. 2. Initial execution at initiator

4.1   Initial Execution

The execution of a transaction t at t's initiator is described in Fig. 2. The operations in t are executed sequentially, and we assume local concurrency control
using locks.

When all operations of t have been executed, t is submitted for ordering and
validation. The list of executed operations is logged, and the read set and write
set (including written values) can be retrieved. The initiator determines the observers for t and initiates the ordering protocol by multicasting *informObservers*

to those observers. This message contains the write set of t which is used to acquire locks for the relevant items. Furthermore, the validating process is notified by the message $validateRequest$, which also contains $WVal(t)$, the updated values, and the mapping $RVer(t)$, associating every item i in $RS(t)$ to the id of the transaction performing the most recent update on i prior to t's read. Note that the initiator may be an observer, and often also the validator.

After the ordering and validation messages are sent, the initiator waits for the commit decision, and replies to the client accordingly. Finally, locks are released.

4.2 Ordering

Figure 3 describes the rules for ordering transactions. Whenever an observer receives an $informObserver$ message for transaction t (rule $INIT\text{-}ORDER$), it creates a $remote\ subtransaction$ to apply t's updates (unless this observer is the initiator). Remote subtransactions are write-only, request high priority locks to abort any local transaction (these would eventually fail validation anyway), and await the commit decision of t before committing. A node for t is also added to the order graph.

The rule $ORDERED$ is executed at process p when a transaction t satisfies the requirements to be $ordered$ at p; i.e., all expected order requests have been received and there are no preceding transactions in the local ordering graph. Then, t is appended to the local order at p and a $propagateOrder$-message is sent to p's parent in the validation hierarchy. Since we use FIFO-unicast, the ordering of $propagateOrder$-messages from process p_a to p_b reflects the local order at p_a.

The rule $RCV\text{-}ORDER$ is executed whenever a process p receives a $propagateOrder$ message for t from a child p' in the validation hierarchy. Unless t is already known at p, the process p first initiates a remote subtransaction to acquire the necessary write locks. In any case, an edge from t_{prev} to t is added to the local order graph of p, where t_{prev} is the most recent transaction received from p' before t. If the ordering becomes inconsistent, there will be a cycle in the local order graph and the transaction is aborted. This rule will be triggered repeatedly for t until all expected $propagateOrder$ messages have arrived. Eventually, t will either be aborted or satisfy the conditions for the rule $ORDERED$ at p; the proposed ordering is then propagated to p's parent.

4.3 Validation

The rule for validation is given in Fig. 4. For each transaction t, validation is performed by the receiver of the $validateRequest$. Validation of t occurs as soon as t has been ordered at p_v and p_v has received the $validateRequest$ message for t. The validation test is a standard optimistic validation procedure, using the local update history at p_v to verify that for each item i read by t, t saw the most recent version of i according to p_v's local order.

RULE: *INIT-ORDER*
when *receive message informObserver(t, WS(t)) from p_{init} to p* **do**
    $Wseq(t)$ = createEmptySeqnumMap()
    if $p =/= p_{init}$ **then** newRemoteSubtransaction(t, $WS(t)$)
    insert (t, $WS(t)$, $Wseq(t)$) **into** *REMOTE-TRANS*
    addNodeToOrderGraph(t,*order-graph*)

RULE: *ORDERED*
when *all order requests received for t at p and predecessors(t, order-graph) == ∅* **do**
    $(WS(t), Wseq(t))$ = getTrans(t, *REMOTE-TRANS*)
    append t **to** *LOCAL-ORDER*
    foreach i **in** $WS(t)$ **do**
        if *hasAllObserversInSubtree(i, p)* **then**
            $seqnum_i$ = incrementLocalSeqnum(i)
            append (i → item-seqnum) **to** $Wseq(t)$
    q = getParent(p)
    if $q \neq nil$ **then** **fifoUnicast** propagateOrder(t, p_{init}, $WS(t)$, $Wseq(t)$) **to** q
    removeFromOrderGraph(t)

RULE: *RCV-ORDER*
when *receive message propagateOrder(tid, p_{init}, WS(t), Wseq(t)) from p* **do**
    if *not* t ∈ *REMOTE-TRANS* **then**
        addNodeToOrderGraph(t, *order-graph*)
        newRemoteSubtransaction(t, $WS(t)$)
    addEdgeToOrderGraph(t,p, *order-graph*)
    if *hasCycle(order-graph)* **then** **broadCast** abort(t)

func *hasAllObserversInSubtree(i : item id, p : process id)*
    return *true* iff p is the lowest process in the validation hierarchy where all observers for i are
    in the subtree rooted by p;

func *newRemoteSubtransaction(t : transaction id, WS(t))*
    applyRemoteUpdatesWithHighPriorityLocks(t, $WS(t)$, *DATABASE*);

Fig. 3. Ordering

5 Performance Evaluation

We have implemented a simulation model using the Real-Time Maude tool, and compared FLACS to a "classical" approach where one master process acts as the central validator. The latter approach was previously shown to outperform protocols that use atomic broadcast in wide-area networks [12]. Since recent research focuses on atomic broadcast-based replica control or weaker consistency models, this comparison is relevant to evaluate the performance of FLACS.

5.1 Experiment Setup

Our experiment setup is an imaginary international travel agent, providing hotel bookings in Paris, New York, London, and Los Angeles. Each city is served by one process, and each process maintains a complete copy of the database. *Scenario A* is a setting with a master validating all transactions. *Scenario B* is our FLACS model, where we assign as observer for an item i the process most likely to access i. We assume a validation hierarchy and network setup as shown in Fig. 5. We model a network with stochastic delay with average values

RULE: *VALIDATION*
when *hasLocalOrder(t) and hasReceivedValidationRequest(t)* **do**
   | **if** *isValid(RS(t), RVer(t), WS(t))* **then broadCast** commit$(t, WS(t), WVal(t), Wseq(t))$
   | **else broadCast** abort(t)
func *isValid(RS(t), RVer(t), WS(t))*
   | **foreach** *i* in *RS(t)* **do**
      | version = getVersion$(i, RVer(i))$
      | **if** *version* < *getLatestVersion(i, DATABASE)* **then** return *false*
   | return *true*

Fig. 4. Validation

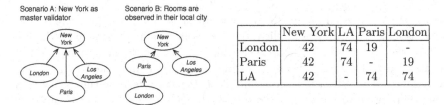

	New York	LA	Paris	London
London	42	74	19	-
Paris	42	74	-	19
LA	42	-	74	74

Scenario A: New York as master validator

Scenario B: Rooms are observed in their local city

Fig. 5. Validation hierarchy with observer placement, and average network delay (ms)

chosen according to the geographical distance.[1] We inject transactions with a *load generator* per process, which generates transaction requests at random times with an adjustable average rate, measured in *transactions per second (TPS)*. All processes have the same average. Once a lock is acquired, we assume a delay of 2 ms per local operation. We do not model protocol overhead since network latency is the dominating factor. In these experiments, no failures are injected.

Each item represents one hotel room at some date. We assume a "hotspot" setting (e.g., a sale period) with only 10 items at each process. We have different transaction types, and each transaction type will access either one room in one city or two rooms (total) in two cities. Each load generator randomly selects a transaction type according to the distribution given in Table 1. The rooms accessed are chosen randomly, and *Book London* represents a read and consecutive write of one room in London. Correspondingly, *Book London+Paris* is the read and consecutive write of one room in London and then one in Paris. We performed four experiments, varying the overall target throughput between 20 and 60 transactions per second. We measured the abort rate and transaction latency, i.e., the time between a request is submitted and it is successfully returned.

5.2   Results

The abort rate and average transaction latency for Scenarios A and B are shown in Fig. 6. Decentralized validation allows FLACS to commit a significantly higher

---

[1] The delays New York–Paris and New York–London are the same, assuming transatlantic backbone links from each of these cities. The delay between Paris and London reflect that network equipment and local lines increase delivery times.

Table 1. Distribution of transaction types per city

New York		Los Angeles		London		Paris	
Book NY	80%	Book LA	80%	Book London	80%	Book Paris	80%
Book Paris	10%	Book NY	10%	Book Paris	10%	Book London	10%
Book NY+LA	10%	Book NY+LA	5%	Book NY+London	5%	Book London+Paris	5%
		Book London+Paris	5%	Book London+Paris	5%	Book NY+London	5%

number of transactions, and the observed transaction latency, affecting both abort rate and user experience, is significantly lower where observers are distributed. This is as expected: In Scenario A, all processes except New York have an average of 84 ms added latency before commit. This increases the delay from an update is initiated until it is applied to other replicas, and consequently, there is a higher probability for transactions elsewhere to read stale data. In Scenario B, the abort rate for transactions accessing items from multiple locations is relatively high. Especially the transaction *Book London+Paris* initiated in Los Angeles suffers, with an abort rate close to 54% at 60 TPS, it should be noted that our experiment is an extreme scenario with only 10 items per city, which greatly increase the chance of conflicts. Figure 7 shows the abort rate per process for both scenarios. In Scenario A, the validation site has significantly lower abort rate than other processes, while in Scenario B, the aborts are more evenly distributed. In FLACS, observer placement and the validation hierarchy are crucial parameters, and in a real system, the observer mapping would benefit from historical data on access patterns, and possibly also semi- or fully-automatized

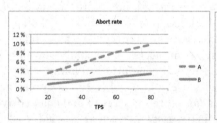
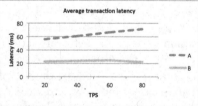

Fig. 6. Abort rate

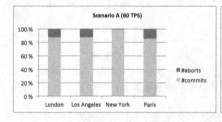
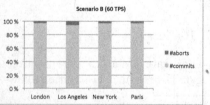

Fig. 7. Commits vs. aborts, per process

dynamic reconfiguration. The general rule is that observers for items commonly accessed together should be close in the validation hierarchy.

6   Related Work

Most recent proposals for efficient data storage in cloud systems are based on decentralization with partitioning. In ElasTraS [4], transactions spanning partitions are only allowed as short transactions with predeclared read sets and write sets. *Megastore* [6] assumes a relatively fine-grained partitioning of the data set, and replicates each partition across a subset of servers. Consistency is achieved by running Paxos within each partition. *Spinnaker* [5] coordinates updates in the same way as Megastore, but executes consistent reads directly at the leader of each partition. Although more fault-tolerant than FLACS, they do not provide consistency across partitions (Megastore provides two-phase commit, but without serializability).

In a wide-area setting, approaches based on *atomic multicast* have been limited by the message delay required to order every update among all processes. The protocols in [13,14] build upon atomic multicast, but they target a wide area setting through partial replication, requiring message ordering only within the group of replicas that together manage the read sets and write sets of the transaction. This differs from FLACS since FLACS allows full replication, but only requires coordination among a limited set of participants (the observers).

Many real-world systems are deployed on top of non-transactional data stores such as Amazon's Dynamo [1] and Cassandra [2]. Both provide *eventual consistency* by committing updates with synchronization among only a subset of participating sites, and the new values are then propagated among other replicas in the background. Updates are *versioned* using vector clocks, and in the case of conflicts updates are reconciled by the application. Although efficient, lacking transactions is a significant disadvantage for systems managing critical data such as audit records, reservations, or financial data.

Microsoft's Azure [15] and Google's Spanner [8] also provide large-scale transactions for cloud applications. Azure is known to give good performance [16] through a master-slave approach, but publicly available details are scarce. Compared to FLACS the transaction latency of any master-based approach will be worse for clients far from the master site, since every update transaction needs at least one message exchange with the master. Spanner provides both high availability through Paxos, replication across wide area networks, and consistency through Multi Version Concurrency Control (using global timestamps). But Spanner is hard to deploy; one obstacle for widespread adoption is that to provide global timestamps, Spanner depends on precisely synchronized clocks and demands a relatively complex infrastructure involving GPS hardware and atomic clocks. Our approach with logical ordering through the validation hierarchy provides a simpler, more generic solution.

7 Conclusion

We have defined a new approach to ensure consistency in cloud-based database systems. The main features of our approach are a method for incremental ordering and a distributed hierarchical validation procedure. Together, these features allow most transactions to be validated near or at the originating site.

We have formalized the entire protocol in Real-Time Maude, and our Real-Time Maude simulations show, as expected, that this approach outperforms a more classical approach where validation takes place at centralized master site.

A number of systems for cloud-based data management use Paxos for high availability. We believe FLACS could be combined with one of these, e.g., Megastore, to provide both high availability and consistency across partitions.

References

1. DeCandia, G., et al.: Dynamo: Amazon's highly available key-value store. SIGOPS Oper. Syst. Rev. 41, 205–220 (2007)
2. Lakshman, A., Malik, P.: Cassandra: a decentralized structured storage system. SIGOPS Oper. Syst. Rev. 44, 35–40 (2010)
3. Chang, F.: et al.: Bigtable: A distributed storage system for structured data. ACM Trans. Comput. Syst. 26, 4:1–4:26 (2008)
4. Das, S., Agrawal, D., Abbadi, A.E.: ElasTraS: An elastic transactional data store in the cloud. In: USENIX HotCloud. USENIX (2009)
5. Rao, J., Shekita, E.J., Tata, S.: Using Paxos to build a scalable, consistent, and highly available datastore. Proc. VLDB Endow. 4(4), 243–254 (2011)
6. Baker, J., et al.: Megastore: Providing scalable, highly available storage for interactive services. In: CIDR (2011), http://www.cidrdb.org/cidr2011/Papers/CIDR11_Paper32.pdf
7. Stonebraker, M., Cattell, R.: 10 rules for scalable performance in 'simple operation' datastores. Commun. ACM 54(6), 72–80 (2011)
8. Corbett, J.C., et al.: Spanner: Google's globally-distributed database. In: OSDI 2012, pp. 251–264. USENIX Association, Berkeley (2012)
9. Ölveczky, P.C., Meseguer, J.: Semantics and pragmatics of Real-Time Maude. Higher-Order and Symbolic Computation 20(1-2), 161–196 (2007)
10. Kemme, B., Alonso, G.: Don't be lazy, be consistent: Postgres-R, A new way to implement database replication. In: VLDB 2000 (2000), http://www.vldb.org/
11. Pedone, F., Guerraoui, R., Schiper, A.: The database state machine approach. In: Distributed Parallel Databases (2003)
12. Grov, J., et al.: A pragmatic protocol for database replication in interconnected clusters. In: PRDC 2006. IEEE Computer Society (2006)
13. Sutra, P., Shapiro, M.: Fault-tolerant partial replication in large-scale database systems. In: Luque, E., Margalef, T., Benítez, D. (eds.) Euro-Par 2008. LNCS, vol. 5168, pp. 404–413. Springer, Heidelberg (2008)
14. Schiper, N., Sutra, P., Pedone, F.: P-store: Genuine partial replication in wide area networks. In: SRDS 2010. IEEE (2010)
15. Campbell, D.G., Kakivaya, G., Ellis, N.: Extreme scale with full SQL language support in Microsoft SQL Azure. In: SIGMOD 2010, 1021–1024. ACM (2010)
16. Kossmann, D., Kraska, T., Loesing, S.: An evaluation of alternative architectures for transaction processing in the cloud. In: SIGMOD 2010. ACM (2010)

A Distributed Publish/Subscribe System
for RDF Data

Laurent Pellegrino, Fabrice Huet, Françoise Baude, and Amjad Alshabani

INRIA-I3S-CNRS, University of Nice-Sophia Antipolis
2004 Route des Lucioles, Sophia Antipolis, France
`firstname.lastname@inria.fr`

Abstract. The pub/sub communication style is a prevalent messaging
pattern for filtering information from distributed and large-scale network
(e.g., from the real-time web, sensor networks, etc.) thanks to the decou-
pling between publishers and subscribers. At the same time, persisting
the published information is a prerequisite for any further batch analyt-
ics on such big amount of data. As data can be heterogeneous, reliance
on format from the semantic web such as RDF is unavoidable. In this
paper we introduce two versions of a content-based pub/sub matching
algorithm for RDF described events, working on an adapted version of
the CAN structured P2P network designed to both store and dissemi-
nate RDF events. In contrary to existing pub/sub solutions based upon
structured overlay networks that index semantic events several times due
to the use of hash functions, we leverage the lexicographic order of the
event elements. Thus, only subscriptions and not publications have to be
duplicated, which is better given that in real settings, publications may
occur more frequently than subscriptions. Furthermore, our system allows to publish events made of any number of elements and the subscription language leverages the SPARQL query language. The first algorithm
we introduce initially derives from the ideas discussed by Liarou. et al.
based upon rewriting continuous queries along matching RDF elements
(CSBV) with the purpose to perform the matching between subscriptions
and several RDF elements on multiple nodes. The experimental results
discuss the applicability of the presented algorithms to some synthetic
scenarios and identify, accordingly, which pub/sub matching algorithm
is the more relevant.

1 Introduction

The advent of the Semantic Web by the precursor Tim Bernes-Lee incites available information on the World Wide Web to become more and more structured.
Structured contents are possible thanks to powerful data models such as Resource Description Model (RDF) that makes knowledges machine-processable
and machine-understandable. Many centralized solutions such as Jena [4], Sesame
[1] or OWLIM [11] have been proposed the last years to store and retrieve RDF
data. However, they all suffer from their inherent design that is not suitable to
scale with the perpetual increase of the resources available on the Web. Some

A. Hameurlain, W. Rahayu, and D. Taniar (Eds.): Globe 2013, LNCS 8059, pp. 39–50, 2013.

decentralized approaches have been introduced to overcome this limitation. Most of them relies on Peer-to-Peer (P2P) networks that are recognized as a key communication model to build distributed and reliable applications at very large scale [10]. Usually, structured P2P protocols are provided with a standard abstraction called Distributed Hash Table (DHT) that offers a simple *put(key, value)* and *get(key)* API to store and fetch data. Even though such an abstraction is really well suited for manipulating key/value pairs, it does not support complex queries such as conjunctives and range queries that are at the core of SPARQL [17], the main query language for RDF data. Furthermore, the traditional query/response model is not designed for processing data streams.

Publish/subscribe systems are a natural extension of one-time queries where users formulate meaningful inquiries about their concern and wait for an answer. Unlike one-time queries that are synchronous, pub/sub systems assume that users register their needs through subscriptions also dubbed continuous-queries. As the name suggests, continuous-queries are resolved as soon as incoming information or events match subscribers' interests. Events are published to a brokering network in charge of performing the matching between the publications and the subscriptions that have been registered. Once an event is matched, a notification is triggered to the subscriber(s). Thus, users are kept updated efficiently and gradually.

In this paper we focus mainly on the synergy between RDF-based P2P systems and the pub/sub messaging paradigm. Section 2 gives an overview of the existing works regarding this context. In Section 3 we introduce our data and subscription model along with our system properties. Section 4 enters into the details of the matching algorithms we have developped. Then, we bring out some information about the implementation before to introduce and discuss the experimental results in Section 5. Finally, Section 6 concludes.

2 Related Works

The last two decades, the flexibility, modularity and responsiveness of pub/sub led to the emergence of several solutions. These systems are classified into *topic-based* or *content-based* categories according to their expressivity. Tibco [23] and Pubsubhubbub [7] are representatives of this former category that provides limited filtering capabilities. Most prominent solutions regarding the latter category are certainly Siena [5] and Hermes [16]. Siena, uses *covering-based* routing algorithms to reduce routing entries and unnecessary forwarding of subscriptions. However it incurs several drawbacks that are intrinsic to the choice of the routing algorithm but also the topology that is static and non-structured. Subscriptions are flooded to the whole network and an unsubscribe operation may implicitly unsubscribe to all the filters that are covered by the former filter. Hermes relies on an extension of Pastry [20], a structured P2P protocol named PAN. Subscriptions and publications are sent to a rendez-vous node and notifications are forwarded by using reverse paths. More recently, BlueDove [13] propose to match publications with subscriptions atop a modified version of Cassandra [12] in just one hop: replicating subscriptions on a selected subset of one hop away accessible peers and then selecting one of these replica to trigger the matching according to load information of peers, regularly exchanged throughout the system. The closest system to our is certainly Meghdoot [9]. The authors leverage the CAN [19] logical topology as we do. However, event types, domain (e.g, from 1 to 100 for event type integer) and the maximum number of attributes per event should be defined at startup. Moreover, the initial CAN configuration strongly depends on this last parameter.

RDFPeers [3] is a distributed RDF repository where peers are self-organized into a Multi-Attribute Addressable Network (MAAN) [2]. MAAN extends Chord [22] such that information retrieval may be performed for any triple term. Publishing a triple implies to index it three times, each one based on the hash value of its subject, predicate and object value. Atomic, disjunctive and range subscriptions are supported with the exception of some patterns. For instance, it is not possible to subscribe for all the information nor with some join constraints. Besides, RDFPeers ignores popular terms such as *rdf:type* predicates and, therefore, subscriptions involving them cannot be resolved.

In [18], Ranger et al. introduce an information sharing platform for disseminating RDF activities. Their solution relies on the Scribe [6] system that offers a topic-based pub/sub system on top of Pastry. Queries are expressed in a SPARQL dialect and registered as topics. Unlike other solutions, the algorithm they propose does not index data a priori. Instead, their strategy relies upon finding results through multicast trees built from scratch, associated with redundant caching and cached lookups mechanisms. The peers participating to the propagation are responsible for removing duplicate results within the limit of their buffer. This probably leading to duplicate notifications over the time.

CSBV [14] proposes a generic and DHT agnostic approach for resolving atomic and conjunctive SPARQL subscriptions. Their scheme strongly relies on hashing and requires to index each triple seven times. Owing to the fact that the number of indexations that is required correspond to the combination without repetition of the elements contained by the tuples that are published, it grows quickly up to 15 when quadruples are considered. Subscriptions are resolved by rewriting dynamically subscription patterns matching new incoming publications. The matching algorithm we introduce in the next sections derives from this idea.

Recently, Shvartzshnaider et al. proposed in [21] to combine AI and Peer-to-Peer research approaches for building a pub/sub system that supports publication of arbitrary tuples and subscriptions with standing graph queries. Their idea consists in applying Rete [8] algorithms on a Chord network to resolve join conditions contained by subscriptions. Basically, a Rete network acts as a distributed cache, where subscription patterns that are executed, and also their results are cached for future reuse. Thus, only the changed data are matched against subscriptions. Publications and subscriptions are indexed similarly to RDFPeers in order to create rendezvous nodes where the satisfaction of subscriptions is verified. Although they claim that Rete approach is effective, no discussion is given about how duplicates are avoided when in-memory buffers overflow. Moreover, subscriptions are formulated through an ad-hoc scripting language and no experimental evaluation is available.

3   EventCloud Design

In this section we give a description of the data and subscription model used by our system, dubbed EventCloud. We explain how events and more specifically how RDF data, along with subscriptions, are indexed in a CAN network.

3.1   Data and Subscription Model

Our data and subscription model follows the approach taken in [15] to allow users to formulate queries and subscriptions but also to insert and publish information with the same models, that is respectively RDF and SPARQL.

Events. The data are expressed in the RDF model using 4-tuples (quadruples) whose elements are named RDF terms. In our system an RDF term may be either an IRI or a Literal value. Elements generated at the same time by a given source form a *Compound Event (CE)*, as defined by (1b). Each CE is made of a list of quadruples and all quadruples share a common term called graph value. This term is built with a combination of a unique source identifier and a timestamp. The purpose of this graph value is twofold. It is used to identify the event source, the event itself and also to offer the possibility to link together several quadruples for emulating, yet unbounded, multi-attribute values like in traditional pub/sub systems.

$$q = (g, s, p, o) \mid g, s, p, o \in RDFTerm \qquad (1a)$$
$$CE = (q_1, ..., q_i, ..., q_n) \mid q_i = (g, s_i, p_i, o_i) \qquad (1b)$$

The EventCloud is based on a four dimensional CAN overlay that uses the lexicographic order for routing requests. The four dimensions of the CAN coordinate space are mapped respectively to the graph, the subject, the predicate and the object of any RDF 4-tuple that is indexed. One benefit of this approach is that a quadruple represents a point in the four dimensional Cartesian space. Hence a quadruple will only be stored by a single peer of the overlay. This indexing approach has several advantages. First, it supports range queries (looking for values in a specified range) efficiently. Second, the lexicographic order preserves the data semantics so that is gives a form of clustering of quadruples sharing a common prefix. In contrast, hash-based approaches destroy the natural ordering of information and make the management of complex queries difficult and expensive. The Figure 1 shows how CEs and subscriptions are mapped to a CAN network.

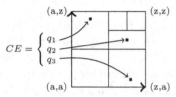
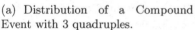

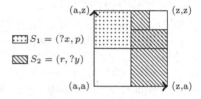

(a) Distribution of a Compound Event with 3 quadruples.

(b) Distribution of 2 subscriptions, overlapping on a peer.

Fig. 1. Example data and subscription distribution on a 2D CAN

Subscriptions. A subscription is content-based and formulated using a subset of SPARQL. It is basically a list of atomic queries called *sub-subscriptions* or *SS* with possibly a FILTER clause. A subscription is applied on different CEs independently, i.e. only the quadruples that belong to the same *CE* can trigger a notification. More precisely, a subscription $S = \{SS_1, SS_2, ..., SS_n\}$ is found to match a *Compound Event* $CE = \{q_1, q_2, ..., q_m\}$ if for each SS_i there exists at least a matching q_j. In other words, the whole subscription should be matched by a subset of the quadruples contained by a CE.

```
1    PREFIX foaf: <http://xmlns.com/foaf/0.1/>
2    SELECT ?id ?name WHERE {
3        GRAPH ?g {
4            ?id foaf:name ?name .    // the point at the end of line
5            ?id foaf:age ?age        // stands for the and operator
6        }
7        FILTER (?age > 25)
8    }
```

Listing 1.1. Example of a SPARQL subscription

For instance, the example depicted in Listing 1.1 states that all events that are related to an entity, with a name and whose age is greater than 25, have to be delivered to the subscriber.

To index the subscription in the overlay, we use a similar scheme than for the events. The subscription is transformed into a set of RDF quadruples. This set is made of the first sub-subscription and additional quadruples. The first one contains a unique identifier, the second one a timestamp and the last one the whole subscription. This set is then sent to the peers responsible for the fixed parts of the first sub-subscription. The subscription presented in the previous example is decomposed as shown in Listing 1.2 and S will be stored on the peers responsible for *?id foaf:name ?name*, i.e. those with a zone with value *foaf:name* on the predicate dimension, and any value on all others (graph, subject and object).

```
1    S = { (?g, ?id, foaf:name , ?name),
2          (id and timestamp), (subscription) }
```

Listing 1.2. Decomposition of a SPARQL subscription in RDF sets

3.2 System Properties

In addition to the data and subscription model, our framework also enforces a set of properties. If a *Compound Event* is added to the overlay, where there exist a matching subscription, then it will be delivered to the subscriber. Conversely, no *false positive* should be delivered. Finally, the causal ordering of publish and subscribe requests will be maintained for a given client (acting both as publisher and subscriber). If a subscription is issued before a matching compound event by the same client, then a notification should be issued.

4 Publish/Subscribe Algorithms

This section introduces two pub/sub algorithms optimized for different use cases. The first one, named *Chained Semantic Matching Algorithm* (CSMA), is optimized for the publications while *One-step Semantic Matching Algorithm* (OSMA) is optimized for the subscriptions.

4.1 CSMA

The general idea of CSMA, as inspired by Liarou et al., is to publish in parallel and perform the matching of all the sub-subscriptions sequentially. Indeed, all peers involved in a subscription will be organized in a chain-like fashion. Only the peers indexing the subscription, as described in Section 3.1 can start the matching process and notify the next peers in the chain which, in turn, will try to find a match. The process ends when reaching the last peers in the chain, i.e. when the whole subscription is satisfied.

Event Routing: A *Compound Event* upon entering the overlay is divided into simple events and each of them is published independently. There are two situations which can trigger the search for a subscription match.

Event Reception: When receiving an event, a peer checks whether there is a matching subscription or not. If there is one and the current event satisfies the *first* atomic query, then the subscription is rewritten into S'. The rewrite operation consists in replacing the variables of the atomic query with the event elements, basically striping down the subscription of the matched values. It also adds the unique identifier of the *Compound Event* so that the rewritten subscription can only match the remaining events. This new subscription is then sent into the overlay for re-indexing and potential matching.

Subscription Reception: When a peer receives a new subscription, it checks for events generated after the subscription but received before, using the timestamp value. This situation could occur because of events and subscription taking different path in the overlay, but more often because of the rewriting described earlier. Hence, this mechanism will allow for a rewritten subscription to match events from the same *Compound Event*, even if they were received earlier.

Finally, when the last matching is performed, the subscriber is notified about the corresponding graph value and can begin the reconstruction process.

Reconstruction: When notified of the graph value g of a matching *Compound Event*, a subscriber performs a reconstruction operation to retrieve the whole event. It synchronously queries the overlay with $(g, ?s, ?p, ?o)$ quadruple pattern to retrieve all events of the *Compound Event*. Since some events might still be routed to the correct peer in the overlay, we use a timeout based algorithm, i.e. if some events are still missing the subscriber waits a fixed duration before re-issuing a new request.

The main drawback of CSMA is that matching a subscription is essentially a sequential process with a complexity (number of steps) equals to the number of sub-subscriptions. Although any peer in the chain can receive a matching event, an ordering constraint is imposed by the subscription. Hence, we don't take advantage of the distributed nature of the subscription.

Furthermore, CSMA may suffer from duplicate notifications. This can happen when there is not a single peer at the end of the matching chain. For example, if the last sub-subscription, after rewriting, still contains variables, then it will be indexed on multiple peers and potentially trigger multiple notifications. Thus a filtering at subscriber side has to be performed during the reconstruction.

4.2   OSMA

To alleviate the previous issues, we propose a second algorithm, OSMA, which allows for parallel matching of subscriptions.

Routing: Instead of indexing only individual quadruples, we now index the whole *Compound Event* on each peer using each quadruple as a key.

Event Reception: When receiving the whole CE, the peer first stores only the quadruples which fall in its responsibility zone. Then, it looks for the subscriptions satisfied by the whole *Compound Event*.

Notification Triggering: Before notifying the subscriber of a match, some care has to be taken to avoid duplicate notifications. Indeed, potentially all peers storing the subscription and involved in the indexation of quadruples from the CE have now enough information to notify the match. To ensure only one peer sends the notification, we apply the following rule. A peer notifies a match *if and only if* it is responsible for the *first* of the matching events of the CE. For instance, if we have a $CE = (q_1, q_2, q_3)$, a subscription $S = (SS_1)$ and two peers P_1 and P_2 that receive respectively q_2 and q_3 and index both SS_1. If q_2 is the first quadruple from the CE that satisfies SS_1 on P_1, then only P_1 notifies the subscriber.

The main benefit of this algorithm is the expected low latency for subscribers. As soon as the CE reaches the peer responsible for the first matching event, the notification if triggered. Also there is no need for a reconstruction phase because the *Compound Event* can be directly sent to the subscriber. However, this is done at the cost of bandwidth since the whole *Compound Event* is sent to multiple peers. Also, note that this algorithm cannot deal with the situation where a subscription is created before an event but reaches a peer after. Correctly managing this case requires falling back to CSMA, which we do.

To summarize, the different properties of the two algorithms are presented in Table 1.

Table 1. Comparison of the two pub/sub algorithms

	Routed Element	Matching Steps	Duplicates	Happen-Before
CSMA	Individual quadruples	Multiple, Chain-like and Reconstruction	Yes, filtering required	Enforced
OSMA	Whole *Compound Event*	Single	No	Requires CSMA

5   Experiments

The latest version of our system dubbed EventCloud is publicly available[1] as an open source project under the AGPL license. From an implementation point of view each peer embeds Jena TDB instances for data and subscription storage.

The experiments introduced hereafter have been performed on 29 nodes of the Grid'5000 testbed. Each machine embeds a Xeon E5520 @ 2,26 GHz with 32 GB RAM, a hard disk drive at 7200 RPM. The partition used for data storage is an EXT3 partition mounted with options *noatime* and *nobarrier* for performance reasons. Java 7 was used with JVM option *-server*. Each result is the average execution on 6 runs where the first run is laid aside due to JVM warmup.

The workload we are using is made of x synthetic events and y subscriptions that are generated to be distributed uniformly among the available peers. This allows us to evaluate the performance of the algorithms when the number of peers involved is the largest.

Subscriptions are generated to embed k quadruple patterns of the form $(?g, ?s1, p1, ?o1) \wedge (?g, ?o1, p2, ?o2) \wedge \ldots \wedge (?g, ?o_{k-1}, p_k, ?o_k)$. *Compound Events* are generated to evenly match subscriptions.

In the first experiment we evaluate the effect of increasing the network size. For this purpose we place 1 peer per machine and vary the total number of peers from 1 to 25. There is only one subscriber with a subscription made of $k = 5$ patterns. One publisher publishes 3×10^3 CEs, each one containing 5 quadruples for an approximate size of 670 Bytes. Figure 2(a) depicts the average subscriber

---

[1] http://eventcloud.inria.fr

throughput[2], i.e. the throughput perceived on the subscriber when the network size it increased. OSMA outperforms CSMA by a factor of 5.43 according to the median value. This difference is explained by the matching which is performed in one step with OSMA whereas CSMA requires a number of steps equals to the number of SS contained by a subscription that is satisfied. Thus, increasing the number of routing steps required.

In a second experiment we evaluate the effect of varying the number of publications. Figure 2(b) shows that the throughput on the subscriber is constantly increasing with OSMA when the number of publications increases. This is because the overlay is not working at its full capacity when $x = 30 \times 10^3$ CEs are published. On the contrary with CSMA the subscriber throughput decreases quickly with the number of publications. This behavior is explained by the reconstruction process which overloads peers with requests, slowing the insertions and the notifications. Owing to the reason that the time required to complete the experiments is too large when more than 21000 CEs are published with CSMA, some values are omitted.

The third experiment evaluates the impact of varying the number of subscriptions registered in the system. The scenario consists in one subscriber subscribing with various number of subscriptions. The subscriptions are generated to match an equal number of *Compound Events*. Figure 2(c) shows the subscriber throughput for 1 to 60 subscriptions. With OSMA the throughput decreases almost linearly with the number of subscriptions in the system. The reason lies in the indexing of the subscription. Since it relies on the first sub-subscription which contains only a predicate as fixed term, only half of the peers of the overlay are actually participating in the matching. Also, some of them have multiple subscriptions to check for each *Compound Event* received, which is a costly operation with Jena TDB. On the contrary, CSMA remains almost stable with a throughput that varies around 92 CEs per second. This effect is explained by the rewritten subscriptions that are generated once a first sub-subscription is satisfied. A rewritten subscription contains in our case more fixed parts than its parent and is indexed against potentially less and different peers, thus, increasing the number of peers involved in the matching.

In a fourth experiment we test the effect of varying the number of peers when selective subscriptions are replaced by a subscription that accepts all events (c.f. Figure 2(d)). In such a situation, all peers index the subscription SELECT ?g WHERE { GRAPH ?g { ?s ?p ?o }}. As explained in Section 4.1, CSMA generates a lot of duplicate notifications in this situation, which limits the scalability. Since OSMA always performs a single notification, the throughput increases with the number of peers.

Finally, the time taken to store different number of publications with no subscription registered on peers is depicted on Figure 2(e). This criteria is directly related to the bandwidth consumption since no matching is performed. Indeed,

---

[2] Mathematically speaking it is defined as the number of matching publications divided by the time elapsed between the first notification and the last awaited notification received by the subscriber.

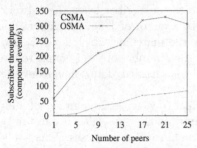

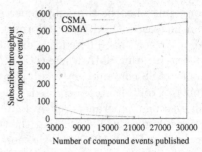

(a) Impact of overlay size. 3000 CEs published, one subscription of $k = 5$ quadruple patterns.

(b) Impact of the number of publications. 25 peers, one subscription ($k = 5$).

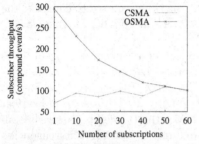

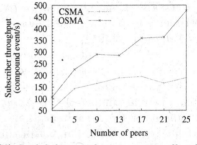

(c) Impact of the number of subscriptions. 25 peers and 3000 CEs published.

(d) Scalability with one accept-all subscription. 3000 CEs published.

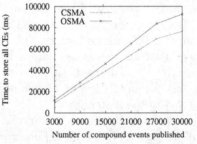

(e) Time to store publications on peers. 25 peers, no subscription, 25 quadruples per CE.

Fig. 2. Performance comparison of CSMA and OSMA

the only difference between the two algorithms with this configuration is the quantity of information conveyed from peers to peers. The time to store the published events quickly differs between CSMA and OSMA when the number of publications increases from 3000 to 30000. It confirms that OSMA requires more time than CSMA to forward events to peers that are responsibles to store quadruples. Thus, it will require more bandwidth than CSMA.

In conclusion, the experiments show that OSMA outperforms CSMA in terms of throughput and scalability at the cost of a higher bandwidth consumption. Its only limitation is that it cannot enforce the happen-before relation and hence, depending on the use case, some applications will have to rely on CSMA.

6   Conclusion

In this paper we have introduced a pub/sub framework based on the RDF data model and SPARQL filter model. Subscribers can express their interests using the SPARQL language and events are published as RDF data. We rely on a multi-dimensional indexing space and lexicographical order to distribute both the publications and subscriptions on an overlay. Compared to previous works, our scheme does not require multiple indexing of the same publication, thus reducing the storage space. We have proposed two algorithms for matching subscriptions. The first one, CSMA, is based on the canonical chain-like approach. It reduces the bandwidth used when publishing at the cost of a longer matching time. It can also handle ordering issues which can happen when the same client submits both publications and subscriptions. The second one, OSMA, uses a fully distributed approach which leads to good performance at the cost of a slightly heavier publication process. Both algorithms have been experimentally tested for throughput and scalability.

Acknowledgments. This work was in part supported by the EU FP7 STREP project PLAY and French ANR project SocEDA. Experiments presented in this paper were carried out using the Grid'5000 experimental testbed (see https://www.grid5000.fr). The authors wish to thank Bastien Sauvan, Iyad Alshabani, Justine Rochas and Maeva Antoine for their help with the implementation.

References

1. Broekstra, J., Kampman, A., van Harmelen, F.: Sesame: A generic architecture for storing and querying RDF and RDF schema. In: Horrocks, I., Hendler, J. (eds.) ISWC 2002. LNCS, vol. 2342, pp. 54–68. Springer, Heidelberg (2002)
2. Cai, M., Frank, M., Chen, J., Szekely, P.: Maan: A multi-attribute addressable network for grid information services. Journal of Grid Computing 2(1), 3–14 (2004)
3. Cai, M., Frank, M., Yan, B., MacGregor, R.: A subscribable peer-to-peer rdf repository for distributed metadata management. Web Semantics: Science, Services and Agents on the World Wide Web 2(2), 109–130 (2004)
4. Carroll, J., Dickinson, I., Dollin, C., Reynolds, D., Seaborne, A., Wilkinson, K.: Jena: implementing the semantic web recommendations. In: Proceedings of the 13th International World Wide Web Conference on Alternate Track Papers & Posters, pp. 74–83. ACM (2004)
5. Carzaniga, A., Rosenblum, D., Wolf, A.: Design and evaluation of a wide-area event notification service. ACM Transactions on Computer Systems (TOCS) 19(3), 332–383 (2001)

6. Castro, M., Druschel, P., Kermarrec, A., Rowstron, A.: Scribe: A large-scale and decentralized application-level multicast infrastructure. IEEE Journal on Selected Areas in Communications 20(8), 1489–1499 (2002)

7. Fitzpatrick, B., Slatkin, B., Atkins, M.: Pubsubhubbub protocol (2010), http://pubsubhubbub.googlecode.com/svn/trunk/pubsubhubbub-core-0.3.html

8. Forgy, C.L.: Rete: A fast algorithm for the many pattern/many object pattern match problem. Artificial Intelligence 19(1), 17–37 (1982), http://dx.doi.org/10.1016/0004-3702(82)90020-0

9. Gupta, A., Sahin, O.D., Agrawal, D.P., El Abbadi, A.: Meghdoot: Content-based publish/Subscribe over P2P networks. In: Jacobsen, H.-A. (ed.) Middleware 2004. LNCS, vol. 3231, pp. 254–273. Springer, Heidelberg (2004)

10. Jelasity, M., Kermarrec, A.M.: Ordered slicing of very large-scale overlay networks. In: Sixth IEEE International Conference on Peer-to-Peer Computing, P2P 2006, pp. 117–124. IEEE (2006)

11. Kiryakov, A., Ognyanov, D., Manov, D.: OWLIM – A pragmatic semantic repository for OWL. In: Dean, M., Guo, Y., Jun, W., Kaschek, R., Krishnaswamy, S., Pan, Z., Sheng, Q.Z. (eds.) WISE 2005 Workshops. LNCS, vol. 3807, pp. 182–192. Springer, Heidelberg (2005)

12. Lakshman, A., Malik, P.: Cassandra decentralized structured storage system. Operating Systems Review 44(2), 35 (2010)

13. Li, M., Ye, F., Kim, M., Chen, H., Lei, H.: A scalable and elastic publish/subscribe service. In: 2011 IEEE International Parallel & Distributed Processing Symposium (IPDPS), pp. 1254–1265. IEEE (2011)

14. Liarou, E., Idreos, S., Koubarakis, M.: Continuous RDF query processing over DHTs. In: Aberer, K., et al. (eds.) ASWC 2007 and ISWC 2007. LNCS, vol. 4825, pp. 324–339. Springer, Heidelberg (2007)

15. Pellegrino, L., Baude, F., Alshabani, I.: Towards a scalable cloud-based rdf storage offering a pub/sub query service. In: The Third International Conference on Cloud Computing, GRIDs, and Virtualization, pp. 243–246 (2012)

16. Pietzuch, P., Bacon, J.: Hermes: A distributed event-based middleware architecture. In: Proceedings of 22nd International Conference on Distributed Computing Systems Workshops, pp. 611–618. IEEE (2002)

17. Prud Hommeaux, E., Seaborne, A., et al.: Sparql query language for rdf. W3C Recommendation 15 (2008)

18. Ranger, D., Cloutier, J.-F.: Scalable peer-to-peer RDF query algorithm. In: Dean, M., Guo, Y., Jun, W., Kaschek, R., Krishnaswamy, S., Pan, Z., Sheng, Q.Z. (eds.) WISE 2005 Workshops. LNCS, vol. 3807, pp. 266–274. Springer, Heidelberg (2005)

19. Ratnasamy, S., Francis, P., Handley, M., Karp, R., Shenker, S.: A scalable content-addressable network. ACM SIGCOMM Computer Communication Review 31(4), 160–172 (2001)

20. Rowstron, A., Druschel, P.: Pastry: Scalable, decentralized object location, and routing for large-scale peer-to-peer systems. In: Guerraoui, R. (ed.) Middleware 2001. LNCS, vol. 2218, pp. 329–350. Springer, Heidelberg (2001)

21. Shvartzshnaider, Y., Ott, M., Levy, D.: Publish/Subscribe on top of DHT using RETE algorithm. In: Berre, A.J., Gómez-Pérez, A., Tutschku, K., Fensel, D. (eds.) FIS 2010. LNCS, vol. 6369, pp. 20–29. Springer, Heidelberg (2010)

22. Stoica, I., Morris, R., Karger, D., Kaashoek, M., Balakrishnan, H.: Chord: A scalable peer-to-peer lookup service for internet applications. ACM SIGCOMM Computer Communication Review 31(4), 149–160 (2001)

23. TIBCO, I.: Tib/rendezvous white paper, Palo Alto, California (1999)

An Algorithm for Querying Linked Data Using Map-Reduce*

Manolis Gergatsoulis[1], Christos Nomikos[2],
Eleftherios Kalogeros[1], and Matthew Damigos[1]

[1] Database & Information Systems Group (DBIS),
Department of Archives and Library Science, Ionian University, Corfu, Greece
{manolis,kalogero}@ionio.gr, mgdamig@gmail.com
[2] Department of Computer Science, University of Ioannina, Greece
cnomikos@cs.uoi.gr

Abstract. In this paper, we exploit the widely used Map-Reduce framework and propose a generic two-phase, Map-Reduce algorithm for querying large amount of linked data. The algorithm is based on the idea that the data graph can be arbitrarily partitioned into *graph segments* which can be stored in different nodes of a cluster of commodity computers. To answer a user query Q, Q is also decomposed into a set of subqueries. In the first phase, the subqueries are applied to each graph segment, in isolation, and intermediate results are computed. The intermediate results are combined in the second phase to obtain the answers of the query Q. The proposed algorithm computes the answers to a given query correctly, independently of a) the data graph partitioning, b) how graph segments are stored, c) the query decomposition, and d) the algorithm used for calculating (partial) results.

Keywords: Linked Data, Graph Querying, Map-Reduce, Distributed Processing, Cloud Computing, Semantic Web.

1 Introduction

As RDF becomes more widely established and the amount of linked data is rapidly increasing, the efficient querying of large amounts of data becomes a significant challenge. On the other hand, the MapReduce is a programming model, which is based on the definition of two functions, the *Map* and the *Reduce* function, for processing large datasets in a distributed manner.

In this paper, we propose a generic two-phases, Map-Reduce algorithm for querying large amount of linked data. The algorithm is based on the idea that the data graph can be arbitrarily partitioned into *graph segments* which can be stored in different nodes of a cluster of commodity computers. The user poses a query Q to the system, which is also decomposed into a set of subqueries.

---

* This research was supported by the project "Handling Uncertainty in Data Intensive Applications", co-financed by the European Union (European Social Fund - ESF) and Greek national funds, through the Operational Program "Education and Lifelong Learning", under the research funding program THALES.

A. Hameurlain, W. Rahayu, and D. Taniar (Eds.): Globe 2013, LNCS 8059, pp. 51–62, 2013.
© Springer-Verlag Berlin Heidelberg 2013

In the first phase of the algorithm, the subqueries are applied to each segment of the data graph, in isolation, and intermediate results are computed. Then these intermediate results are combined in the second phase of the algorithm to give the answers to the user query Q. The proposed algorithm computes the answers to a given query correctly, independently of: a) the data graph partitioning, b) how graph segments are stored, c) the query decomposition, and d) the algorithm used for calculating (partial) results.

2 Data and Query Graphs

In this section we introduce an abstract version of our data model. For this, we assume two disjoint infinite sets U_{so} and U_p of URI references, an infinite set L of (plain) literals[1], and a set V of variables. A triple $(s, p, o) \in U_{so} \times U_p \times (U_{so} \cup L)$ is called a *data triple*. A triple $(s, p, o) \in (U_{so} \cup V) \times U_p \times (U_{so} \cup L \cup V)$ is called a *query triple*. In a data/query triple, s is said to be the *subject*, p the *predicate* and o the *object*. A *data graph* G is a set of data triples. A *query graph* (or simply a *query*) Q is a set of query triples. The *output pattern* $O(Q)$ of a query Q is the sequence $(X_1, \ldots, X_n)$ of the variables appearing in Q. A data graph G' is a *subgraph* of a data graph G if $G' \subseteq G$. A query Q' is a *subquery* of a query Q if $Q' \subseteq Q$. Note that, data graphs correspond to ground RDF graphs defined in [2,9], i.e. RDF graphs without blank nodes. Graphically, a data/query triple (s, p, o) is represented by $s \xrightarrow{p} o$. A node (subject or object) is represented as a rounded rectangle unless it is literal which is represented by a rectangle. Strings with initial lowercase letters represent predicates, while strings with initial uppercase letters denote URIs. Literals are strings enclosed in double quotes. Finally, we assume that variables' names begin with the question mark symbol (?).

Example 1. Fig. 1(a) (resp. 1(b)) depicts a data (resp. query) graph. □

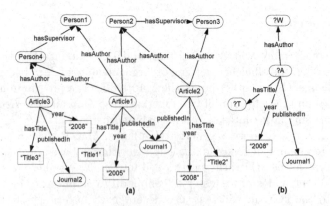

Fig. 1. (a) A data graph, and (b) a query graph

---

[1] In this paper we do not consider typed literals.

The *nodes* $nd(G)$ (resp. $nd(Q)$) of a data graph G (resp. a query graph Q) is the set of elements of $U_{so} \cup L$ (resp. $U_{so} \cup L \cup V$) that occur in the triples of G (resp. Q). The *arc labels* $al(G)$ (resp. $al(Q)$) of a data graph G (resp. a query graph Q) is the set of elements of U_p that occur in the triples of G (resp. Q).

Definition 1. *An (total) embedding of a query graph Q in a data graph G is a total mapping $e : nd(Q) \rightarrow nd(G)$ with the following properties:*

1) For each node $v \in nd(Q)$ either v is a variable or $v = e(v)$.

2) For each triple $(v_1, p, v_2) \in Q$, the triple $(e(v_1), p, e(v_2))$ is in G.

The tuple $(e(X_1), \ldots, e(X_n))$, where $(X_1, \ldots, X_n)$ is the output pattern of Q, is said to be an answer *to the query Q.*

Example 2. Fig. 2 shows an embedding of the query Q in data graph G. The answer obtained is $(?A, ?W, ?T) = (Article2, Person3, "Title2")$. Note that a second embedding exists giving $(?A, ?W, ?T) = (Article2, Person2, "Title2")$. □

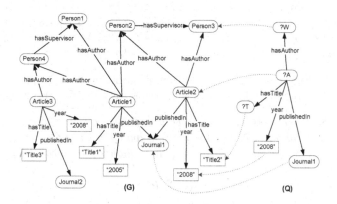

Fig. 2. An embedding of the query graph Q in the data graph G

Definition 2. *A partial embedding of a query graph Q in a data graph G is a partial mapping $e : nd(Q) \rightarrow nd(G)$ such that for every node $v \in nd(Q)$ for which $e(v)$ is defined the following properties hold:*

1) if v is not a variable, then $e(v) = v$.

2) if v is a variable, then there exists a node $u \in nd(Q)$ for which $e(u)$ is defined and an arc label $p \in al(Q)$, such that $(v, p, u) \in Q$ and $(e(v), p, e(u)) \in G$ or $(u, p, v) \in Q$ and $(e(u), p, e(v)) \in G$.

A partial embedding is non-trivial *if there is a triple $(v_1, p, v_2) \in Q$ such that both $e(v_1)$ and $e(v_2)$ are defined and the triple $(e(v_1), p, e(v_2))$ belongs to G.*

Definition 3. *Two partial mappings $e_1 : D_1 \rightarrow R_1$ and $e_2 : D_2 \rightarrow R_2$ are said to be* compatible *if for every $v \in D_1 \cap D_2$ such that $e_1(v)$ and $e_2(v)$ are defined,* it is $e_1(v) = e_2(v)$. *The join of two compatible partial mappings e_1 and e_2 is the partial mapping $e : D_1 \cup D_2 \to R_1 \cup R_2$ defined as follows:*

$$e(v) = \begin{cases} e_1(v) & \text{if } e_1(v) \text{ is defined} \\ e_2(v) & \text{if } e_2(v) \text{ is defined and } e_1(v) \text{ is undefined} \\ \text{undefined} & \text{if both } e_1(v) \text{ and } e_2(v) \text{ are undefined} \end{cases}$$

Definition 3 applies also to partial embeddings as they are partial mappings. It is trivial to prove that the join of two compatible partial embeddings is a partial embedding and that the join operation is commutative and associative.

3   Data Graph Partitioning

In this section we define the notion of the partition of a data graph.

Definition 4. *An m-triple partition of a data graph G is a an m-tuple $\mathcal{P} = (G_1, \ldots, G_m)$ where $G_1, \ldots, G_m \subseteq G$, such that $\bigcup_i G_i = G$ and $G_i \cap G_j = \emptyset$, for all i, j, with $1 \leq i < j \leq m$. Each subgraph $G_1, \ldots, G_m$ is called graph segment. A border node v of G_i, is a node that belongs to $nd(G_i) \cap nd(G_j) \cap U_{so}$ for some $j \neq i$. We denote by $B(G_i)$ the set of border nodes of G_i.*

Example 3. In Fig. 3 we see a 3-triple partition of the data graph G of Fig. 1. The dark nodes correspond to the border nodes between the graph segments.   □

Definition 5. *Let $\mathcal{P} = (G_1, \ldots, G_m)$ be a m-triple partition of a data graph G and let e be a partial embedding of a query graph Q in some G_i. Then e is called a usefull partial embedding of Q in G_i if the following conditions hold:*

(a) e is non-trivial.

(b) for each node $v \in (nd(Q) \cap nd(G_i))$ that is not a variable, $e(v)$ is defined.

(c) for each triple $(v, p, u) \in Q$, if $e(v)$ is defined and $e(v) \notin (B(G_i) \cup L)$, then $e(u)$ is also defined and $(e(v), p, e(u))$ is a triple in G_i.

(d) for each triple $(v, p, u) \in Q$, if $e(u)$ is defined and $e(u) \notin (B(G_i) \cup L)$, then $e(v)$ is also defined and $(e(v), p, e(u))$ is a triple in G_i.

Notice that, if v is a non-variable node in Q that maps to a non-border element of G_i, the second property implies that $e(v)$ is defined, and the third and fourth property enforce every triple that contains v to be mapped in G_i.

Example 4. Consider the query graph Q appearing in the left part of Fig. 4. This query graph represents the query: *"Find the articles (variable ?A) and their title (variable ?T) published in Journal1 which have as author a person (variable ?P1) and his supervisor (variable ?P2)".* It is easy to see that the evaluation of this query on the data graph G appearing in Fig. 1 returns the answers:

Answer 1: $(?P1, ?A, ?P2, ?T) = (Person4, Article1, Person1, \text{“Title1”})$.

Answer 2: $(?P1, ?A, ?P2, ?T) = (Person2, Article2, Person3, \text{“Title2”})$.

Now, if we partition G as shown in Fig. 3, we cannot evaluate Q on a single graph segment. Instead, all segments G_1, G_2 and G_3 are needed to evaluate Q (by joining the appropriate partial embeddings of Q in G_1, G_2 and G_3).   □

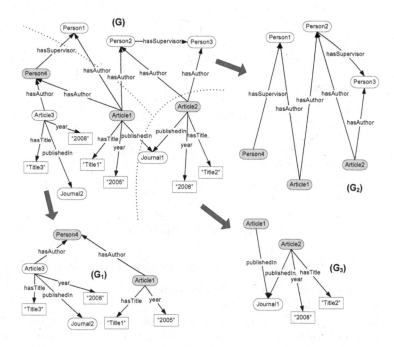

Fig. 3. 3-triple partition of the data graph G of Fig. 1

4   Query Decomposition

In this section we show that in order to find the answers to a query Q, it suffices to decompose Q into a set of subqueries $\{Q_1, \ldots, Q_m\}$, find the answers of $\{Q_1, \ldots, Q_m\}$ and then to join them to find the answer to Q.

Definition 6. *A decomposition of a query Q is a n-tuple $\mathcal{F} = (Q_1, \ldots, Q_n)$ such that $Q_1, \ldots, Q_n \subseteq Q$ and $\bigcup_i Q_i = Q$. $\mathcal{F}$ is non-redundant if $Q_i \cap Q_j = \emptyset$ for all i, j with $1 \leq i < j \leq n$. A branching node in Q is a node in $nd(Q_i) \cap nd(Q_j)$ for a pair i, j, where $i \neq j$. $B(Q)$ denotes all branching nodes of Q.*

Theorem 1. *Let $\mathcal{F} = (Q_1, \ldots, Q_n)$ be a query decomposition of a query graph Q and $\mathcal{P} = (G_1, \ldots, G_m)$ be a m-triple partition of a data graph G. Then the following statements are equivalent:*

1. *e is a total embedding of Q in G.*
2. *for every j, with $1 \leq j \leq n$, there exist useful partial embeddings $e_{j,1}, \ldots, e_{j,k_j}$ of Q_j in $G_{i_{j,1}}, \ldots, G_{i_{j,k_j}}$ for some $i_{j,1}, \ldots, i_{j,k_j}$ with $1 \leq i_{j,1} < \ldots < i_{j,k_j} \leq m$ that satisfy the following properties:*
   (a) for every j, with $1 \leq j \leq n$, and every triple $(v, p, u) \in Q_j$ there exists some ℓ such that $e_{j,\ell}(v)$, $e_{j,\ell}(u)$ are defined and $(e_{j,\ell}(v), p, e_{j,\ell}(u)) \in G_{i_{j,\ell}}$.
   (b) for every j_1, j_2, ℓ_1, ℓ_2, with $1 \leq j_1 \leq j_2 \leq n$, $1 \leq \ell_1 \leq k_{j_1}$, $1 \leq \ell_2 \leq k_{j_2}$, the partial embeddings e_{j_1,ℓ_1} and e_{j_2,ℓ_2} are compatible.
   (c) the join of e_{j,ℓ_j} for all $j \in \{1, \ldots, n\}$ and all $\ell_j \in \{1, \ldots, k_j\}$ is e.

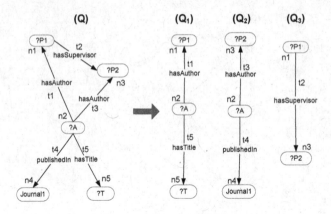

Fig. 4. Query decomposition

Theorem 1 suggests the following general query evaluation strategy:

Step 1: Decompose the data graph G into a set $\mathcal{P} = (G_1, \ldots, G_m)$ of segments that are stored in different computer nodes.

Step 2: Decompose the query Q into a set of subqueries $\mathcal{F} = (Q_1, \ldots, Q_n)$.

Step 3: Compute locally (at each node keeping a segment G_i) all possible useful partial embeddings of each subquery Q_j.

Step 4: For each subquery Q_j, collect and join the partial embeddings of Q_j obtained in Step 3 to get total embeddings of Q_j.

Step 5: To construct the total embeddings (i.e. answers) of Q join the total embeddings obtained in Step 4 by using one embedding for each subquery.

Example 5. (Continued from Example 4) Consider the decomposition of the query Q appearing in the right part of Fig. 4. The answers appearing in Example 4 can be found by applying queries Q_1, Q_2 and Q_3 on segments G_1, G_2 and G_3 and joining the embeddings obtained in this way.   □

5   An Algorithm to Answer Queries Using Map-Reduce

In this section we present an algorithm which implements the query evaluation strategy, presented in Section 4, on the MapReduce programming framework.

5.1   MapReduce Framework

MapReduce is a programming model for processing large datasets in a distributed manner. The storage layer for the MapReduce framework is a Distributed File System (DFS), such as Hadoop Distributed File System (HDFS), and is characterized by the block size which is typically 16-128MB in most of DFSs. Creating a MapReduce job is straightforward. The user defines two functions, the *Map* and the *Reduce* function, which run in each cluster node, in isolation. The map function is applied on one or more files, in DFS, and results [key,value] pairs. This process is called *Map task*. The nodes that run the Map tasks are called *Mappers*. The *master controller* is responsible to route the pairs to the *Reducers* (i.e., the nodes that apply the reduce function on the pairs) such that all pairs with the same key initialize a single reduce process, called *reduce task*. The reduce tasks apply the reduce function in the input pairs and also results [key,value] pairs. This procedure describes one *MapReduce step*. Furthermore, the output of the reducer can be set as the input of a map function, which gives to the user the flexibility to create procedures of multiple steps.

5.2 The Preprocessing Phase

For the presentation of the algorithm we assume the following:

- Three numbering functions I_t, I_b and I_{nb} assign unique integer IDs to triples (from 1 to $|Q|$), to branching nodes (from 1 to $|B(Q)|$), and to non-branching nodes (from 1 to $|nd(Q) - B(Q)|$), of the query Q, respectively.
- We construct: a) a list BN of the branching nodes of Q, b) a list NBN of the non-branching nodes of Q, and c) a list *tripleList* of the triples in Q.
- Q is decomposed into $Q_1, \ldots, Q_n$. Each Q_i is related to a *query prototype* $(bnFlags, nbnFlags, tFlags)$ where $bnFlags$, $nbnFlags$ and $tFlags$ have one place for each branching node, non-branching node, and triple in Q, respectively, to denote its presence (denoted by "+") or absence (denoted by "-") in Q_i. We also construct a set $NBL = \{(b_i, Q_j)| \ b_i \in BN$ and $b_i \notin nd(Q_j)\}$.
- A (partial) embedding e of a (sub)query is represented as a triple of tuples $(BNt, NBNt, tF)$. BNt (resp. $NBNt$) stores the images of branching (resp. non-branching) nodes of Q. An asterisks ('*') is placed in the corresponding node place if it is not defined in e. Finally, tF keeps tracks for the triples taking place in e (by putting a '+' sign in the corresponding place of tF).

Preprocessing phase emits the above to the mappers of Phase 1 with key the pair $(subqueryID, SegmentID)$. NBL is emitted to all reducers of Phase 1.

Example 6. (Continued from Example 5). The preprocessing phase constructs: the subqueries Q_1, Q_2, and Q_3, the list of branching nodes $BN = (n1, n2, n3)$, the list of non-branching nodes $NBN = (n4, n5)$, the list of triples $tripleList = (t1, t2, t3, t4, t5)$, the list of missing branching nodes $NBL = \{(n1, Q2), (n2, Q3), (n3, Q1)\}$, and the (sub)query prototypes:

Q_1: (<+,+,_>, <_,+>, <+,_,_,_,+>)
Q_2: (<_,+,+>, <+,_>, <_,_,+,+,_>)
Q_3: (<+,_,+>, <_,_>, <_,+,_,_,_>)   □

5.3 Phase 1 of the Algorithm

Mapper of Phase 1. The mapper gets a subquery Q_i and a graph segment G_j, evaluates Q_i on G_j and returns all useful (total and partial) embeddings which emits to the reducers of Phase 1 with key the subquery ID Q_i:

mapper1$((Q_i, G_j), (GjData, subqueryInfo))$
$//(Q_i,G_j): Q_i/G_j$ is the ID of a subquery/data segment
$// GjData$: the content of the data graph segment G_j
$// SubqueryInfo$: prototypes/branching & non-branching nodes/triples of Q
begin
    - compute $E = \{e|e$ is a useful partial embedding of Q_i in GjData$\}$
    - **for each** $e \in E$ **do** emit $([Q_i, e])$
end.

Example 7. (Continued from Example 6). Some embeddings of Q_1, Q_2 and Q_3 in the segments G_1, G_2 and G_3 computed by the corresponding mappers and emitted with key the subquery ID, appear below. More specifically, a total embedding evaluated and emitted by *the mapper working on* (Q_1, G_1), is[2]:

(1)   key = Q1, value = (<Person4,Article1,*>, <*,"Title1">, <+,-,-,-,+>)

The *Mapper working on* (Q_2, G_1) computes and emits the partial embedding:

(2)   key = Q2, value = (<*,Article1,Person4>, <*,*>, <-,-,+,-,->)

Between the embeddings obtained and emitted by *the Mapper working on* (Q_1, G_2) is the (partial) embedding:

(3)   key = Q1, value = (<Person2,Article2,*>, <*,*>, <+,-,-,-,->)

Between the embeddings obtained and emitted by the *Mapper working on* (Q_2, G_2) are the (partial) embeddings:

(4)   key = Q2, value = (<*,Article1,Person1>, <*,*>, <-,-,+,-,->)

(5)   key = Q2, value = (<*,Article2,Person3>, <*,*>, <-,-,+,-,->)

The *Mapper working on* (Q_3, G_2) computes and emits the total embeddings:

(6)   key = Q3, value = (<Person4,*,Person1>, <*,*>, <-,+,-,-,->)

(7)   key = Q3, value = (<Person2,*,Person3>, <*,*>, <-,+,-,-,->)

The *Mapper working on* (Q_1, G_3) emits the partial embedding:

(8)   key = Q1, value = (<*,Article2,*>, <*,"Title2">, <-,-,-,-,+>)

The *Mapper working on* (Q_2, G_3) emits the partial embeddings:

(9)   key = Q2, value = (<*,Article1,*>, <Journal1,*>, <-,-,-,+,->)

(10)   key = Q2, value = (<*,Article2,*>, <Journal1,*>, <-,-,-,+,->)

The mappers working on (Q_3, G_3) and (Q_3, G_1) return no embeddings.   □

Reducer of Phase 1. A reducer receives all useful embeddings of a subquery Q_i in all graph segments $G_1, \ldots, G_m$ of G, computes all total embeddings of Q_i, in G and emits them to the mappers of phase 2 with key the subquery ID. It also emits (with proper subquery IDs as keys) the branching node values from the total embeddings of Q_i to be used in the total embeddings of other subqueries:

reducer1$(Q_i, values)$
$// Q_i$: a subquery ID. values: contains a list of embeddings for Q_i and the NBL list
begin
    - collect in a list F_i the total embeddings of Q_i appearing in values or
       obtained by joining partial embeddings in values
    - **for each** embedding $e = (bn, nbn, tl)$ in F_i **do**

---

[2] Notice that we can check if an embedding is total or partial by comparing it with the corresponding subquery prototype (see Example 6).

begin
 - emit($[Q_i,\ (bn,\ nbn)]$); // *emits total embedding with key the subquery Q_i*
 - **for** $i = 0$ **to** $|bn|$-1 **do**
  if $(bn[i] \mathrel{!=} \text{'*'})$ **then**
   for each (i, Q_j) in NBL **do** emit($[Q_j, (i, bn[i])]$);
 end
end.

Example 8. (Continued from Example 7). Between the total embeddings of Q_1 that constructs and emits *reducer with key Q_1* are:
(1)=> key = Q1, value = (<Person4,Article1,*>, <*,"Title1">)
(3)+(8)=> key = Q1, value = (<Person2,Article2,*>, <*,"Title2">)
It also emits the following missing branching node values:
key = Q2, value = (1,Person2) key = Q2, value = (1,Person4)
key = Q3, value = (2,Article1) key = Q3, value = (2,Article2), ...
The *Reducer for key $Q2$* constructs and emits the total embeddings for Q_2:
(4)+(9)=> key = Q2, value = (<*,Article1,Person1>, <Journal1,*>)
(5)+(10)=> key = Q2, value = (<*,Article2,Person3>, <Journal1,*>)
and the following values for missing branching nodes:
key = Q3, value = (2,Article1) key = Q3, value = (2,Article2)
key = Q1, value = (3,Person1) key = Q1, value = (3,Person3), ...
Reducer for key $Q3$ emits:
(6)=> key = Q3, value = (<Person4,*,Person1>, <*,*>)
(7)=> key = Q3, value = (<Person2,*,Person3>, <*,*>)
key = Q2, value = (1,Person2) key = Q2, value = (1,Person4)
key = Q1, value = (3,Person1) key = Q1, value = (3,Person3) □

5.4 Phase 2 of the Algorithm

Mapper of Phase 2. Each mapper manipulates the embeddings of a specific subquery. It fills in their missing branching node values using values from the embeddings of other subqueries and emits the resulted embeddings to the reducers of Phase 2 (the key is the tuple of the branching node values):

mapper2(Q_i, *values*)
// Q_i: *the ID of a subquery*
// *values: a set E of the parts (bn, nbn) of the total embeddings of Q_i and*
// *a set V of pairs (i, v), where v is a candidate value for $bn[i]$*
begin
 - **for each** embedding $e = (bn, nbn)$ in E **do**
  - **for each** instance bn' of bn using the values in V **do** emit($[bn', (Q_i, nbn)]$)
end.

Example 9. (Continued from Example 8). *Mapper with key Q1 receives:*

E = {(<Person4,Article1,*>, <*,"Title1">), (<Person2,Article2,*>, <*,"Title2">),...}
V = {(3,Person1), (3,Person3),... }

This mapper produces instances of the branching node tuples in E by replacing the '*' in the 3rd place with a value in V. Between the key-value pairs obtained and emitted in this way are:

key = (Person4,Article1,Person1), value = (Q1, <*,"Title1">)
key = (Person2,Article2,Person3), value = (Q1, <*,"Title2">)
The input of the *Mapper with key Q2* is:
E = {(<*,Article1,Person1>, <Journal1,*>),
    (<*,Article2,Person3>, <Journal1,*>), ... }
V = {(1,Person2), (1,Person4), ...}
Some of the instances that this mapper produces and emitted are:
key = (Person4,Article1,Person1), value = (Q2, <Journal1,*>)
key = (Person2,Article2,Person3), value = (Q2, <Journal1,*>)
The input of the *Mapper with key Q3* is:
E = { (<Person4,*,Person1>, <*,*>), (<Person2,*,Person3>, <*,*>) }
V = {(2,Article1), (2,Article2)}
Some key-value pairs produced and emitted (as above) by this mapper are:
key = (Person4,Article1,Person1), value = (Q3, <*,*>)
key = (Person2,Article2,Person3), value = (Q3, <*,*>)   □

Reducer of Phase 2. In each reducer, the embeddings (one for each subquery in $(Q_1,\ldots,Q_n)$) are joined[3] to construct the final answers of Q:

reducer2(key, values)
// key: a tuple of branching node values
// values: pairs of the form (Q_i, partial embedding for non-branching nodes)
begin
  - **for each** join obtained by using one embedding for each subquery **do**
      - Emit the result produced by this join
end.

Example 10. (Continued from Example 9). The *Reducer with key (Person4, Article1, Person1)* receives the set {(Q1, <*,"Title1">), (Q2, <Journal1,*>), (Q3, <*,*>)}, joins these embeddings and returns the answer:
<Person4,Article1,Person1,Journal1,"Title1">
The *reducer with key (Person2,Article2,Person3)* receives the set {(Q1, <*, "Title2">), (Q2, <Journal1,*>), (Q3, <*,*>)} which joins giving the answer:
<Person2,Article2,Person3,Journal1,"Title2">
Notice that no other reducer returns solution (as they do not receive embeddings for all subqueries).   □

5.5   Implementation of the Algorithm

An experimental implementation of our algorithm has been developed using Hadoop 1.0.4. For our experiments we have used a cluster of 14 nodes of the following characteristics: Intel Pentium(R) Dual-Core CPU E5700 3.00GHz with

---

[3] Notice that the joined embeddings are, by construction, compatible.

4GB RAM. The datasets used have been obtained and adapted from the Lehigh University Benchmark (LUBM)[4]. Each graph segment has been stored in a different node of the cluster, in a relational MySQL database whose schema consists of two tables, one containing the triples of the segment and the other containing the border nodes. Partial embeddings have been obtained by transforming each (sub)query graph into an equivalent SQL query and applying it to the segment stored in the database. Three different datasets of size shown in Fig. 5 have been used in our experiments. The datasets have been randomly split into 14 segments of equal size and stored in the MySQL databases of the cluster nodes. Each one of the first three queries consists of 6 triples and contains 3 different

Dataset Size	query 1	query 2	query 3	query 4	query 5	AVG
113,6Mb	3,15	4,06	3,47	4,25	3,17	3,62
231,6Mb	4,11	4,57	4,38	5,55	3,53	4,43
491,5Mb	8,24	9,44	9,03	10,37	5,06	8,43

Fig. 5. Execution times (in mins) of 5 different queries in 3 different datasets

variables, while each one of the last two queries consists of 4 triples and contains 2 different variables. Each query has been decomposed into 3 (query 1, 4 and 5) or 4 subqueries (query 2 and 3). Each subquery contains at least one URI reference or literal in a triple's subject or object. The execution times seems encouraging. However, more excessive experiments, with different number of nodes in the cluster are planed for the near future.

6 Related Work

During the last few years, several methods for answering SPARQL queries using the MapReduce model have been proposed. The method in [6] works for any partition of the RDF data. Given a query, one MapReduce job selects the relevant triples and a sequence of MapReduce jobs perform multiway joins. In [4] the RDF triples are stored in multiple HDFS files, according to their predicates and objects. For each query, only the relevant files are read from the disk.

In [3] the RDF graph is vertex partitioned and its parts are stored with some triple replication, to ensure that for small queries, each answer can be computed using a single part of the graph. Larger queries are decomposed and the answers to the subqueries are joined by MapReduce jobs. In HadoopRDF [1], RDF triples with the same predicate are placed in the same part of the data graph, which is stored in a traditional triple store, such as Sesame. Queries are divided in the same way, so that each subquery can be answered by a single computer-node. The answers to the subqueries are merged by MapReduce jobs.

In H_2RDF system [8] data triples are stored in HBase. In order to answer a query, a sequence of joins is executed, which is obtained in a greedy manner. Other methods have been proposed, which translate SPARQL queries to other query languages, such as JACL ([7]) and PigLatin ([5], [10]).

---

[4] http://swat.cse.lehigh.edu/projects/lubm/

7   Conclusion

In this paper, we presented a generic algorithm, based on the MapReduce frame-work, for querying large amount of linked data. Compared to the methods that have been proposed in the literature, the novel feature of our approach is that it is based on the notion of partial embedding, that allows the local computation of the largest possible fragment of each answer (by taking benefit of well-known methods for centralized SPARQL query answering); MapReduce is used only to combine fragments obtained in various nodes.

Note that, our algorithm does not allow queries with variables in the place of predicates. However, it is easy to extend the algorithm to allow such variables. Notice also that, we assumed that (see Definition 4), a data triple cannot belong to two different graph segments. However, the proposed algorithm can also be applied to segments that violate this restriction.

Finally, note that the proposed algorithm is independent of the data partition-ing and storing, the query decomposition, and the algorithm used for calculating (partial) results. However, there are interesting problems to investigate, such as how to partition the triples so as to minimize the number of border nodes or the cost of evaluating queries.

References

1. Du, J.-H., Wang, H.-F., Ni, Y., Yu, Y.: HadoopRDF: A scalable semantic data analytical engine. In: Huang, D.-S., Ma, J., Jo, K.-H., Gromiha, M.M. (eds.) ICIC 2012. LNCS, vol. 7390, pp. 633–641. Springer, Heidelberg (2012)
2. Gutierrez, C., Hurtado, C.A., Mendelzon, A.O., Pérez, J.: Foundations of semantic web databases. J. Comput. Syst. Sci. 77(3), 520–541 (2011)
3. Huang, J., Abadi, D.J., Ren, K.: Scalable SPARQL querying of large RDF graphs. PVLDB 4(11), 1123–1134 (2011)
4. Husain, M.F., Khan, L., Kantarcioglu, M., Thuraisingham, B.M.: Data intensive query processing for large RDF graphs using cloud computing tools. In: Proc. of CLOUD 2010, pp. 1–10. IEEE (2010)
5. Mika, P., Tummarello, G.: Web semantics in the clouds. IEEE Intelligent Systems 23(5), 82–87 (2008)
6. Myung, J., Yeon, J., Goo Lee, S.: SPARQL basic graph pattern processing with iterative mapreduce. In: Proc. of MDAC. ACM (2010)
7. Nie, Z., Du, F., Chen, Y., Du, X., Xu, L.: Efficient SPARQL query processing in MapReduce through data partitioning and indexing. In: Sheng, Q.Z., Wang, G., Jensen, C.S., Xu, G. (eds.) APWeb 2012. LNCS, vol. 7235, pp. 628–635. Springer, Heidelberg (2012)
8. Papailiou, N., Konstantinou, I., Tsoumakos, D., Koziris, N.: H2RDF: adaptive query processing on RDF data in the cloud. In: Proc. of WWW 2012 (Companion Volume), pp. 397–400. ACM (2012)
9. Pérez, J., Arenas, M., Gutierrez, C.: Semantics and complexity of SPARQL. ACM Trans. Database Syst. 34(3) (2009)
10. Schätzle, A., Przyjaciel-Zablocki, M., Lausen, G.: PigSPARQL: mapping SPARQL to Pig Latin. In: SWIM (2011)

Effects of Network Structure Improvement
on Distributed RDF Querying

Liaquat Ali, Thomas Janson, Georg Lausen, and Christian Schindelhauer

University of Freiburg
{ali,janson,lausen,schindel}@informatik.uni-freiburg.de
http://www.informatik.uni-freiburg.de

Abstract. In this paper, we analyze the performance of distributed RDF systems in a peer-to-peer (P2P) environment. We compare the performance of P2P networks based on Distributed Hash Tables (DHTs) and search-tree based networks. Our simulations show a performance boost of factor 2 when using search-tree based networks. This is achieved by grouping related data in branches of the tree, which tend to be accessed combined in a query, e.g. data of a university domain is in one branch. We observe a strongly unbalanced data distribution when indexing the RDF triples by subject, predicate, and object, which raises the question of scalability for huge data sets, e.g. peer responsible for predicate 'type' is overloaded. However, we show how to exploit this unbalanced data distribution, and how we can speed up the evaluation of queries dramatically with only a few additional routing links, so-called *shortcuts*, to these frequently occurring triples components. These routing shortcuts can be established with only a constant increase of the peer's routing tables. To cope with hotspots of unfair load balancing, we propose a novel indexing scheme where triples are indexed 'six instead of three times' with only 23% data overhead in experiments and the possibility of more parallelism in query processing. For experiments, we use the LUBM data set and benchmark queries.

1 Introduction

A goal of the Semantic Web [1] initiative is to integrate data from web resources into machine-driven evaluation. The Resource Description Framework (RDF [2]) data model has been proposed by the W3C to encode these data. To cope with the anticipated load of the Semantic Web data, several projects have emerged that have studied distributed solutions for the storage and querying of RDF data. State-of-the-art distributed RDF data stores such as RDFPeers [3], Atlas [4,5], and BabelPeers [6] use Distributed Hash Tables (DHTs) to store and query RDF data in a distributed manner. To attain an efficient search for RDF triples with the same subject, predicate, or object, the triples are indexed three times for each triple component (subject, predicate, or object) in these distributed RDF databases. DHTs while provide fair load balancing properties with easy data

A. Hameurlain, W. Rahayu, and D. Taniar (Eds.): Globe 2013, LNCS 8059, pp. 63–74, 2013.

management under churn[1] they also destroy the ordering of the index by using hashing, and along with it the grouping of semantically-related data, e.g. data of a university domain cannot be stored on a contiguous interval and is spread over the complete table. This can cause more routing when collecting data from the same domain to evaluate a query.

GridVine [7] and our proposed distributed RDF system 3rdf [8] address this by using the P2P networks P-Grid [9] and 3nuts [10] respectively, providing a distributed search tree for order-preserving indexing. Domain-related prefixes (namespaces) in subjects, predicates, and objects of RDF triples order triples of the same domain in the same branches of the search tree. In return, the data belonging to the same domain is stored on nearby peers (in the metric of the overlay routing structure) or even at the same peer.

In this paper, we evaluate the performance of distributed RDF systems when using either the Chord or 3nuts P2P-network and when using two different RDF data distributions in the network, the state-of-the-art indexing for subject, predicate, and object and a novel indexing introduced in this paper. In Section 2 we provide an overview about distributed RDF systems and distributed query evaluation techniques relating to this work. In Section 3 we present our simulation including overlay networks, RDF data and query model, data distribution including our new indexing scheme for a fairer data distribution, and the query processing including speed-ups by exploiting additional features of the 3nuts network. Based on this simulator, the simulation results regarding the performance of the RDF system with the performance metrics routing-steps and time for RDF query evaluation are presented in Section 4. Finally, we conclude in Section 5, and give a brief outlook on future work.

2   Related Work

With more and more Web resources annotated with RDF information, distributed solutions for storage and querying of RDF data is a need. Several projects have proposed peer-to-peer networks for the distributed evaluation of RDF data. The majority of these projects, such as RDFPeers [3], Atlas [4,5], and BabelPeers [6], use DHTs for the storage and querying of RDF data. The basic idea here is to store each triple at three locations using the hash values of subject, predicate, and object. Triples with a specific subject, predicate, or object are obtained during query evaluation by computing the hash value of that specific key again to resolve the peer providing these triples. To improve the query load distribution, authors in [5] additionally index the triples by combinations of triple components 'subject+predicate', 'subject+object', 'predicate+object', and 'subject+predicate+object', with 7 replications of each triple in total. In Section 3.3 we present a similar technique but with another objective, which offers a more balanced data distribution. In the work [3] they measure the amount of highly frequent triple components. The authors of [3,6] mention that triples

---

[1] Peers entering/leaving the network only invoke local changes and take over/shed data to neighbors.

are not distributed uniformly in the network because of non-uniform distributed index-keys. In this paper we will provide an analysis of the data distribution.

Traditional DHT-based P2P networks, such as Chord [11], are used as underlying overlay networks in the aforementioned distributed RDF data stores applying uniform hash functions to map data keys to peers in the network. This achieves good storage load balancing but sacrifices the preservation of the semantic proximity of RDF triples because it destroys existing relations among the inserted triples keys (attributes) based on their order. RDF triple keys which are semantically close at the application level are heavily fragmented in DHTs, and hence the efficiency of RDF range queries or queries posed on semantically-related attributes is significantly spoiled in these networks.

GridVine [7] and 3rdf [8] are other distributed RDF systems proposed for the storage and querying of RDF data. GridVine and 3rdf use the P-Grid [9] and 3nuts [10] P2P networks respectively, to provide an order-preserving search tree instead of a DHT-based search structure. The ordering in the tree can represent the semantical proximity of closely related RDF triples (e.g. triples predicates with the same prefix will be organized in the same subtree). In contrast to P-Grid, 3nuts provides the additional feature of so-called *interest locality*, where peers with a special interest in a particular search key or path can voluntary participate in managing these paths. When co-managing a path and establishing routing there, a peer increases its routing table but retains fast routing in that path with direct links to other peers in the branch of the path. This is the reason why we say the peer has a *shortcut* to that path. Additionally, the peer may also participate in voluntary managing data in a path (which we do not make use of in this work).

3   Simulation

3.1   Network Models

We simulate a distributed RDF system using either the DHT-based overlay Chord or the search-tree based overlay 3nuts and compare the performance between both. The results might be transferable to the complete class of both DHT-based and search-tree based peer-to-peer networks. The basic difference between both will be explained below.

DHT-Based Overlay Networks. The majority of the state-of-the-art distributed RDF systems still use DHTs [12] for data allocation in the distributed system. In a DHT, each peer and data item has an identifier, e.g. network address and file name, which are hashed to a hash key in key space $[0, 2^m)$ for a typical constant $m = 128$ for 128-bit keys. A peer then gets all data assigned which has a hash key between its hash key and the next larger hash key of another peer in the key space ring. It can be shown that the key space range assigned to any peer is not greater than factor $\mathcal{O}(\log n)$ as the expected key space range which is $2^m/n$ for n peers in the network. This results in a fair load balancing of data IDs. The DHT implementations then provide a routing structure to store and look up data items with a lookup time, for instance, for Chord [11] with $\mathcal{O}(\log n)$. Fair load-balancing and logarithmic lookup time achieve scalability where the network performance does not decrease considerably with the size of the network.

Tree-Based Overlay Networks. GridVine and 3rdf are distributed RDF systems using search-tree based overlay networks, such as P-Grid [9] and 3nuts [10]. The fundamental difference when using a search tree instead of a hash table is omitting any hashing of data keys in order to preserves the order of data keys in key space. In addition to logarithmic point queries this achieves efficient range queries in key space, whereas hash tables do not provide an efficient implementation for range queries and the complete table has to be searched. Therefore, when applications such as distributed RDF systems can organize data in key space so that RDF triples needed during query evaluation have nearby keys in key space, (e.g. a similar prefix in the search key equivalent to a small key range), the advantage of range queries can be exploited and lookup time is significantly reduced. The price for efficient range queries in this class of overlays is more complicated and up to a constant factor larger routing structure being more difficult to uphold under churn and data sets with high dynamics.

3.2 RDF Data and Query Model

Each node in the distributed RDF system can publish RDF resources in the network. In RDF, resources are expressed as subject-predicate-object expressions, called triples. The subject in a RDF triple denotes the resource, and the predicate expresses a relationship between the subject and the object. Let U and L represent URIs and Literals, respectively in RDF, a triple $(v_1, v_2, v_3) \in U \times U \times (U \cup L)$ over certain resources U and L is called a *RDF triple* [2]. RDF data can also be represented as graph where subject and object are nodes and the predicates are edges.

RDF resources are normally represented by URIs [2], and resources belonging to a particular application domain usually share common namespaces or prefixes (e.g. the 'Professor', 'name', 'email', and 'teach' keys in triples of Listing 1.1 share a common prefix 'ubd0v0'). Thus, the support of efficient range queries in tree-based overlays, which is equivalent to short lookup times between network keys with the same prefix, achieves short querying time when RDF data with the same prefix is associated in a query (see the example in Listing 1.1).

```
@prefix rdf: <http://www.w3.org/1999/02/22-rdf-syntax-ns#>
@prefix ubd0v0: <http://www.lehigh.edu/zhp2/2004/0401/univ-bench.owl#>
@prefix d0v0: <http://www.Department0.University0.edu#>
d0v0:P3     rdf:type    ubd0v0:Professor.
d0v0:P3     ubd0v0:name    Georg.
d0v0:P3     ubd0v0:email    georg@ub.com.
d0v0:P3     ubd0v0:teach    d0v0:course1.
```

Listing 1.1. RDF triples about a resource *d0v0:P3* encoded in RDF/N3 format

Each node in the distributed RDF system can also pose SPARQL basic graph pattern queries to retrieve the RDF data stored in the system. These basic graph pattern queries are composed of triple patterns. Let U, L, and V represent URIs, Literals, and Variables, a triple $(v_1, v_2, v_3) \in (U \cup V) \times (U \cup V) \times (U \cup V \cup L)$ is called a *SPARQL triple pattern* [13]. We evaluate the system performance, such as response time and routing hops needed per query, by performing conjunctive triple pattern queries in simulated RDF systems with either the Chord or 3nuts overlay. Following [5], a *conjunctive query* Q is a formula:

$$?x_1, \ldots, ?x_n : - (s_1, p_1, o_1) \wedge \cdots \wedge (s_n, p_n, o_n)$$

where $?x_1, \ldots, ?x_n$ are variables and each (s_i, p_i, o_i) is a triple pattern. Each variable x_k appears in at least one triple pattern. These patterns are matched against the input RDF triples to find all assignments of variables to URIs and literals such that all triples of the query can be found in the RDF data-store.

3.3 Data Distribution

SPARQL, as well as the majority of RDF query languages, mainly support constraint search of the triples's subject, predicate, or object values. Thus, as in systems like (RDFPeers, Atlas, and BabelPeer), we index each triple three times using the subject, predicate and object identifier.

The degree of the underlying RDF graph is not limited and predicates occur several times to identify the same type of association between nodes. If we index triples by subject, predicate or object, we group the triples with the same identifier on the same peer, with the advantage that we can perform a constraint search for a specific subject, predicate or object in a local database. The main drawback is that we leverage the load balancing techniques of most overlays because data items with the same key are managed on the same peer. Since the degree of this graph is not limited in any way, the load-balancing might be unfair, so that typically there are lots of 'type'-predicates in most practical RDF graphs only managed by one peer.

To cope with unfair load balancing, we propose another indexing scheme where a triple is indexed for each possible combination of its 2 out of 3 components, giving the $\frac{3!}{(3-2)!} = 6$ combinations subject+predicate, subject+object, predicate+subject, predicate+object, object+subject, object+predicate. This means that, for instance, triples containing the predicate 'type' are subdivided according to all possible classes. Thus, in the example of Listing 1.1 there is one specific peer managing all 'types' with object 'professor' but not necessarily 'types' for other objects. So if we already have a constraint for this object in a query, all triples on this peer are sufficient. Queries where two triple components are unknown become more challenging, when not all data for a specific triple component are on the same peer and have to be collected from many peers. This is equivalent to range queries, which are not practical in DHT-based overlays. We therefore see a trade-off in DHT-based systems with two options, either a more balanced data distribution with 6 indexes but limited functionality (evaluation of triple patterns with only 1 constant is not possible) or all functions but more unbalanced data with the 3 index scheme. In contrast, in a search-tree based system these kinds of range queries are very efficient. To retrieve all triples of a specific predicate with the predicate+object index, we go to an arbitrary peer in the predicate's path in the search-tree and scan the subtree for all predicate-object combinations only using direct routing links.

The data amount in the network is not necessarily twice when doubling the number of indexes. Imagine a predicate's path in the tree managed by a single peer in the 3 indexes scheme. This peer then will manage the same triples in the 6 indexes scheme since all triples for indexes predicate+subject and predicate+object will be in the subtree of the path of the predicate's identifier, and a triple has to be transmitted only once in this case instead of twice for different peers for paths predicate+subject and predicate+object. If m peers are in the path of a triple component, the expected overhead factor of triples is $(2 - 1/m)$.

We have analyzed the distribution of triples in our RDF system with $1,000$ peers and $100,000$ triples. Figure 1 shows the triples managed by the peers in decreasing order to the number of triples per peer, e.g. the peer with rank 1 in Figure 1a has $20,000$ triples. Certainly, in an optimal load balancing, all peers would manage the same amount of triples indicated by the constant function of the mean value. For 3 indexes the mean number of triples managed by a peer

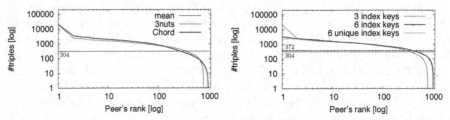

(a) Chrod/3nuts comparison for 3 indexes   (b) #triples/peer in 3nuts for 3/6 indexes

Fig. 1. Triple distribution on peers in distributed RDF system

was 304, but the median peer in 3nuts has 178 triples and in Chord only 132, indicating a slightly better load balancing in 3nuts. When we use 6 instead of 3 indexes (Fig. 1b) and compare the top ranked peers, we can in fact prevent hotspots where peers are overloaded by data and query requests slowing down the system. Surprisingly, the number of triples is only 23% more compared to 3 indexes and (and not 100% more). And, as can be seen in Figure 1b, the peers with only a few triples at the low end for 3 indexes get additional triples in the 6 indexes scheme. Accordingly, the median peer has 279 triples and the mean number of triples is 372 indicating a better distribution than for 3 indexes. We also checked a scheme with 6 indexes but unique ID extensions for all triples to prevent triple clustering. The effect is negligible and the clustering of triples by the same ID does not interfere with load balancing for 6 indexes.

3.4   Query Processing

Data of several peers has to be combined for evaluating conjunctive queries, and we use the query processing algorithm, Query Chain (QC), originally presented in [5], where the triple patterns contained in the query are iteratively resolved by a chain of nodes. The query evaluation starts with a single triple pattern of the query by doing a lookup for the peer responsible for the evaluation of this triple pattern. This peer adds to an intermediate result all triples of its local database qualified for the evaluated triple pattern. The intermediate result is then extended by doing a lookup for a second triple pattern and joining the results. This operation is executed until all triple patterns of the query have been processed.

When triples are indexed six times for good load balancing, the triple storage cost is 23% more for our test data than using three indexes. But we can exploit this extra storage to achieve a better distribution of query processing load and faster query response time by bundling bandwidth with parallelism. The Spread By Value (SBV) query processing, presented in [5], extends the ideas of QC by exploiting the values of matching triples found during processing triple patterns incrementally; it rewrites the next triple pattern and distributes the responsibility of evaluating it to more peers than QC. In our experiment we consider the case where triples are indexed three times, and thus we use QC query processing. Due to the small triple overhead of 23% caused by grouping of data with same data in the same subtree, we will only get parallelism for identifiers of triple components with a large set of triples managed by several peers. But if the number of triples correlates with the result data size, it is not a bad thing.

Exploiting 3nuts Locality Features. The 3nuts *information locality* feature preserves key ordering; therefore for triple patterns with lookup keys sharing the same prefixes (e.g. the 'UndergraduateStudent', 'name', 'advisor', and 'teacherOf' etc lookup keys in Listing 1.2 share a common prefix 'ubd0v0'), the number of hops required to reach all these keys is reduced (at best, some keys are managed by the same peer).

The number of hops required to evaluate triple patterns of a query can be further reduced through a so-called feature *interest locality* provided in the distributed search tree of 3nuts. It allows peers responsible for triples components (subject, predicate, or object) to establish few additional routing links, *shortcuts*, to other frequently occurring components (subject, predicate, or object) of relevant triples. These routing shortcuts can be established with only a constant increase of the peer's routing tables. To support the creation of shortcuts, each peer in the network responsible for the triple components' values (i.e. subject, predicate, or object) creates a link to the peer, sharing at least one of the components' values of the same triple. In this way peers create Peers Link Graph defined as follows:

Definition 1. *A Peers Link Graph G is a tuple (N, E), where N is the set of peers in G and E is the set of directed weighted edges in G. Two peers from N*

are connected with an edge in E if and only if triples managed by these two peers
share at least one triple components' value. The weight of an edge E represents
the frequency of such related triples managed by corresponding peers.

Peers maintain statistics of their weighted links with the help of their locally
stored RDF triples. Each of these Peers Link Graphs is also connected with the
rest of the peers in the network through a directed edge of weight 1.

An example partial Peers Link Graph created for the peers sharing the subjects of triples belonging to the class *Professor* is shown in Figure 2. The edge
from *Peer1* to *Peer3* with weight 2 indicates that 'course1' is taught by two
professors.

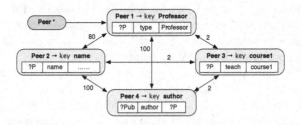

Fig. 2. Example of Peers Link Graph for triples of class Professor

We observe that the frequency of subject, predicate, and object occurrences in
triples is not uniformly distributed, and we can assume that triples components
(subject, predicate, or object) which frequently occur in these triples will also
frequently occur in conjunctive triple pattern queries. We exploit this unbalanced
triple distribution, and thus consider only the top weighted edges of Peers Link
Graph for the creation of *shortcuts*. For example, in Figure 2, the edge from
Peer1 to predicate *name* with weight 80 has a high chance of being considered
for the creation of a shortcut than the edge from *Peer1* to object 'course1' with
weight 2.

4   Performance Analysis

In this section, we present experimental performance evaluation done with a
simulator for our RDF system using either a Chord network or a 3nuts network
and the 3 index scheme presented in Section 3.3 for triple storage in the overlay.
The Java-implemented Simulator includes a simulation for the physical network,
the overlay network, with the distributed RDF system on top. We repeated all
experiments several times but the variation of result values was negligible and is
thus not presented here. For the testing we use the Lehigh University Benchmark
(LUBM [14]) data-set of two universities, each with 16 departments. There were
223, 510 triples in total, which were indexed 3 times in the system. The network
contained up to 16, 285 peers.

Application domains usually mark their own ontologies in RDF data with a unique namespace. Accordingly, each university department in the test set gets a distinctive namespace. In the example Listing 1.1, department 0 of university 0 uses the namespaces 'ubd0v0' and 'd0v0'. We have generated 5 query sets (based on LUBM queries) that sum up to 130 unique queries in total. Each set shares queries of a common structure with distinctive namespaces for each department. The first query set comprises for queries of the type in Listing 1.2 and we vary for instance the namespace 'ubd0v0' for 32 departments to generate more queries.

```
PREFIX  rdf :  <http :// www.w3. org /1999/02/22− rdf−syntax −ns#>
PREFIX  ubd0v0 :  <http :// www. le high . edu/zhp2/2004/0401/univ−bench. owl#>
SELECT  ?std_name  ?teacher_name  ?course_name
WHERE  {  ?X  rdf : type  ubd0v0 : UndergraduateStudent .
?X  ubd0v0 : name  ?std_name .
?X  ubd0v0 : advisor  ?Y.
?Y  ubd0v0 : name  ?teacher_name .
?Y  ubd0v0 : teacherOf  ?Z.
?X  ubd0v0 : takesCourse  ?Z.
?Z  rdf : type  ubd0v0 : Course .
?Z  ubd0v0 : name  ?course_name  }
```

Listing 1.2. SPARQL query returning names of the students their advisors and courses taken, provided that courses taken are taught by their supervisors

4.1   Analysis of Routing

Distributed query processing in a RDF system consists of searching, transferring and evaluating RDF data. The distributed search structure of P2P-networks achieves scalability but slows the search down typically to $\mathcal{O}(\log n)$ routing steps (called hops) in a network with n peers compared to a server with sufficient resources. When the bandwidth of modern networks is high but the ping or delay for data transmission is low, the response time of queries can by driven by these delays, because each routing step in chain produces an additional delay.

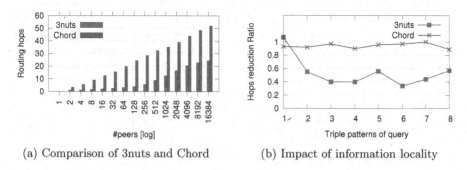

(a) Comparison of 3nuts and Chord   (b) Impact of information locality

Fig. 3. Measurement results for resolving the query in Listing 1.2

Figure 3a shows the mean numbers of hops of lookup-operation for resolving the query of Listing 1.2 depending on the network size n. The linear functions in log-lin scale specially for Chord indicate a logarithmic hop number. The triple components of this query are all in the domain 'ubd0v0'. Consequently, corresponding triples are stored in 3nuts in the same subtree with path 'ubd0v0' and peers managing this subtree have fast lookup to each other. This really keeps the hop numbers down for small networks up to 64 peers where single or only a few peers manage the data for that domain. For larger networks more routing is needed within the subtree and we see a linear increase starting a 128 peers like in Chord.

While Figure 3a showed the total numbers of hops during processing a query, Figure 3b shows the numbers of hops needed for routing of the next triple pattern in chain of triple patterns in the query (percentile to the expected hop numbers $\mathcal{O}(\log n)$). In the Chord overlay, we need almost the same numbers of hops to lookup all indexed triple components. On the contrary, in the 3nuts overlay, the hops for lookup decrease after the first step by 50% and the reason is again the information locality: the first step starts at an arbitrary peer which might not participate in the subtree of domain 'ubd0v0' in the 3nuts tree with $\mathcal{O}(\log n)$ hops, but when the query enters this subtree once, it stays inside for the rest of the query steps with fast routing.

Figure 4b shows further reductions in the numbers of hops needed for evaluating the query in Listing 1.2 with the creation of up to 5 shortcuts by each peer in 3nuts network. If a peer interested in evaluation of a triple pattern maintains a *shortcut* to the lookup key of this triple pattern, then it takes it 0 hops to reach this lookup key. The establishment of constant numbers of shortcuts for each peer to frequently occurring triple components in the network could result to a significant reduction in numbers of hops, e.g. the numbers of hops needed for our example query reduced from 26 to 9 with creation of 4 shortcuts.

4.2   Analysis of Query Response Time

Our simulation does not provide the simulation of a real-world physical network and it is impossible to find one suitable model covering all possible fields of application such as the Internet, Intra net, and so on. Therefore we will present in this section how to derive the query response time from the given experimental routing data with a given physical network model. Let $k = \delta \cdot b$ denote the product of delay δ and bandwidth b in the physical network. The query response time t is then for m triples patterns p_i

$$t = \sum_{i=1}^{m} \left(c_i + \text{hops}_i \cdot \delta + \left(\frac{\text{data}_i \cdot \delta}{k} + \delta \right) \right) \approx \delta \cdot \sum_{i=1}^{m} \left(\text{hops}_i + \frac{\text{data}_i}{b} + 1 \right).$$

where c_i is the computation time for evaluating pattern p_i, hops_i is the number of hops to lookup the peer providing the triples for pattern p_i, and data_i is the data size for triples of pattern p_i to transfer to the next peer. For $c_i \ll \delta$ we neglect the computation time.

The response time is mainly driven by routing delays and data transfer time. When the bandwidth is very high, routing delays are a dominant factor and reducing routing hops with the 3nuts overlay has a big influence, e.g. can reduce the query response time in our example to 65%, see Figure 4a where we calculate the ratio of the query response time for the actual routing of the query and the expected time for an arbitrary routing in the network. The routing in query processing in the Chord overlay almost needs the same time like arbitrary routing steps between arbitrary peers with nearly no effect.

The improvement in query time shown in Figure 4a can be enhanced with the creation of constant numbers of shortcuts to frequently occurring triples components in underlying 3nuts network, e.g. the query time in our example can be further reduced to 30% with creation of 4 shortcuts as shown in the same Figure 4a. The creation of shortcuts reduces traffic and peers routing load as well because a peer maintaining shortcuts to triples components has a direct link to the peers responsible for these components.

Figure 4c shows the ratio of improvements in response time of the query in Listing 1.2 with the creation of up to 5 *shortcuts* by each peer in the 3nuts overlay. The response time of the example query is reduced to 50% with creation of 4 *shortcuts* in the underlying 3nuts overlay.

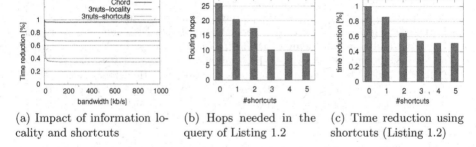

(a) Impact of information locality and shortcuts

(b) Hops needed in the query of Listing 1.2

(c) Time reduction using shortcuts (Listing 1.2)

Fig. 4. Measurement results for the performance boost using 3nuts localities

5   Conclusions

In this paper we analyzed techniques for optimization of distributed RDF systems and showed the practical application by simulation with the benchmark (LUBM) data and queries. We have shown that using search-tree based instead of DHT-based peer-to-peer networks improves the query response time by up to a factor of two if RDF data of the same domain, for instance data of the same university is grouped in the same branch of the tree and the query only combines data of such a limited domain. We also tested the usage of shortcuts in the 3nuts overlay network, where the peers increase their routing structure by a constant factor. This technique achieves a further speed-up of query response times of factor for instance 2.5 for 3 shortcuts per peer. We also presented a novel indexing scheme with 6 indexes which only needs 23% more data in tests compared to the state-of-the-art 3 indexes scheme but improved the load balancing and could eliminate hotspots in the network where peers had to manage far more triples than others, e.g. the predicate 'type'.

References

1. Berners-Lee, T., Hendler, J., Lassila, O.: The Semantic Web. Scientific American 284(5), 34–43 (2001),
   http://www.scientificamerican.com/article.cfm?id=the-semantic-web
2. Klyne, G., Carroll, J.J.: Resource Description Framework (RDF): Concepts and Abstract Syntax. World Wide Web Consortium. Tech. Rep. (2004),
   http://www.w3.org/TR/2004/REC-rdf-concepts-20040210/
3. Cai, M., Frank, M.: RDFPeers: a scalable distributed RDF repository based on a structured peer-to-peer network. In: Proceedings of the 13th International Conference on World Wide Web, New York, USA, pp. 650–657 (2004)
4. Kaoudi, Z., Koubarakis, M., Kyzirakos, K., Miliaraki, I., Magiridou, M., Papadakis-Pesaresi, A.: Atlas: Storing, updating and querying RDF(S) data on top of DHTs. J. Web Sem. 8(4), 271–277 (2010)
5. Liarou, E., Idreos, S., Koubarakis, M.: Evaluating Conjunctive Triple Pattern Queries over Large Structured Overlay Networks. In: Cruz, I., Decker, S., Allemang, D., Preist, C., Schwabe, D., Mika, P., Uschold, M., Aroyo, L.M. (eds.) ISWC 2006. LNCS, vol. 4273, pp. 399–413. Springer, Heidelberg (2006)
6. Battré, D., Heine, F., Höing, A., Kao, O.: On Triple Dissemination, Forward-Chaining, and Load Balancing in DHT Based RDF Stores. In: Moro, G., Bergamaschi, S., Joseph, S., Morin, J.-H., Ouksel, A.M. (eds.) DBISP2P 2005 and DBISP2P 2006. LNCS, vol. 4125, pp. 343–354. Springer, Heidelberg (2007)
7. Aberer, K., Cudré-Mauroux, P., Hauswirth, M., Van Pelt, T.: GridVine: Building Internet-Scale Semantic Overlay Networks. In: McIlraith, S.A., Plexousakis, D., van Harmelen, F. (eds.) ISWC 2004. LNCS, vol. 3298, pp. 107–121. Springer, Heidelberg (2004)
8. Ali, L., Janson, T., Lausen, G.: 3rdf: Storing and Querying RDF Data on Top of the 3nuts Overlay Network. In: 10th International Workshop on Web Semantics (WebS 2011), Toulouse, France, pp. 257–261 (August 2011)
9. Aberer, K.: P-Grid: A Self-Organizing Access Structure for P2P Information Systems. In: Batini, C., Giunchiglia, F., Giorgini, P., Mecella, M. (eds.) CoopIS 2001. LNCS, vol. 2172, pp. 179–194. Springer, Heidelberg (2001)
10. Janson, T., Mahlmann, P., Schindelhauer, C.: A Self-Stabilizing Locality-Aware Peer-to-Peer Network Combining Random Networks, Search Trees, and DHTs. In: ICPADS, pp. 123–130 (2010)
11. Stoica, I., Morris, R., Karger, D., Kaashoek, M.F., Balakrishnan, H.: Chord: A scalable peer-to-peer lookup service for internet applications. SIGCOMM Comput. Commun. Rev. 31, 149–160 (2001)
12. Karger, D., Lehman, E., Leighton, T., Panigrahy, R., Levine, M., Lewin, D.: Consistent Hashing and Random Trees: Distributed Caching Protocols for Relieving Hot Spots on the World Wide Web. In: Proceedings of the 29th Symposium on Theory of Computing (STOC 1997), pp. 654–663. ACM, New York (1997)
13. SPARQL Query Language for RDF, http://www.w3.org/TR/rdf-sparql-query/
14. Guo, Y., Pan, Z., Heflin, J.: LUBM: A Benchmark for OWL Knowledge Base Systems. Web Semantics: Science, Services and Agents on the World Wide Web 3(2-3) (2005)

Deploying a Multi-interface RESTful Application in the Cloud

Erik Albert and Sudarshan S. Chawathe

University of Maine

Abstract. This paper describes the design, implementation, and deployment of an application server whose primary infrastructure is an elastic cloud of servers. The design is based on the Representational State Transfer (REST) style, which provides significant benefits in a cloud environment. The paper also addresses implementation issues within a specific cloud service and highlights key decisions and their effect on scalability and cost. Finally, it describes our experiences in deploying a widely used platform with both Web and mobile client interfaces and its ability to cope with load spikes while maintaining a low quiescent cost.

1 Introduction

There are a number of challenges inherent to the design and deployment of a data-driven Web and mobile application suite, particularly when faced with a severely limited budget and the possibility for unexpected spikes in utilization. Here we describe the design and deployment of the 10Green application infrastructure in the cloud, weigh the pros and cons of several important design options, and highlight the benefit of utilizing a RESTful design approach. Our approach is based on adapting a traditional Web deployment strategy (i.e., single-server and relational database-driven) to establish a strategy that is cost-effective, quick to implement and deploy, highly scalable, and not dependent on large Web service frameworks or (though not incompatible with) specialized cloud database implementations such as Relational Cloud [6] or epiC [4], or services offered through cloud providers such as Amazon RDS and Microsoft SQL Azure.

The 10Green project integrates air quality data available from governmental resources and provides an intuitive interface that summarizes the information in a manner accessible to scientists and non-scientists alike. While the datasets used by the application are already publicly available on the Web, it is often difficult and laborious to obtain, analyze, integrate, and interpret this climatological data. Converting such raw datasets into easily interpreted results requires expertise in file formats, climate science, and other fields, making it essentially inaccessible to most people. The 10Green score for a location is calculated by comparing a year's worth of measured samples of ten important types of airborne pollutants against a set of standard levels based on published health standards. If fewer than twenty percent of the reported measurements exceed the standard,

A. Hameurlain, W. Rahayu, and D. Taniar (Eds.): Globe 2013, LNCS 8059, pp. 75–86, 2013.
© Springer-Verlag Berlin Heidelberg 2013

then the pollutant is rated at the healthy level and contributes to the 10Green score. Pollutants at the unhealthy level or lacking environmental monitoring negatively impact the score. Example score displays are shown in Fig. 1 for both the Web and mobile applications. More inquisitive users can explore deeper into the data, e.g., by viewing how the concentrations of pollutants vary geographically over a map. The 10Green application is currently available on the Web at http://www.10green.org and in the Google Play market[1].

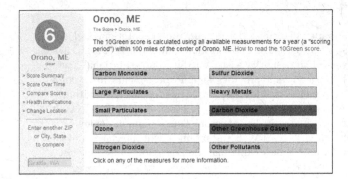

Fig. 1. The 10Green Web and mobile applications

In the following sections we introduce the 10Green application server and give rationale for a design pattern that supports the development of Web and mobile applications that takes full advantage of the parallelism that can be achieved in a cloud environment. Then, we give two deployment strategies for a data-driven application and highlight the properties of the application that would favor one over the other. Finally, we give conclusions and observations on the design and deployment based on experiences with deploying the 10Green application.

2   The Application Server

The 10Green application server (Fig. 2) is the primary computational unit of the 10Green project. The database, which can be hosted externally to the server, stores air quality and scoring data. The Web interface is a standard Web server that hosts the 10Green Web application and site. The application programming interface (API) permits programmatic access to the 10Green data and scores, including a tile mapping service (TMS) that supports the efficient generation maps of climate data. Finally, an internal cache can be used to store the results of dynamically generated content to make future requests more efficient.

2.1   A REST-Based Approach

REST (Representational State Transfer) [7,8,12] is a client-server architectural style that stresses scalability, usability, accessibility, and decentralized growth

---

[1] https://play.google.com/store/apps/details?id=org.tengreen.free

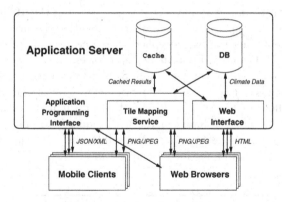

Fig. 2. The application server

as well as allowing for greater design flexibility. The 10Green application server uses a REST-based design for two main reasons: First, REST facilitates rapid and effective scaling of the number of server instances from a single instance to tens or hundreds during periods of high usage. The fundamental principles of the REST style require that clients interact with the server through a standardized interface and that all necessary state is encoded entirely within each transactions made between the client and the server. A request made to the server is not dependent on any implicit state maintained by the server (there is none). Thus, any available server instance can service any incoming request from clients. Scalability is important for the 10Green application, which experiences large spikes in load after media coverage while the average load is very low. Second, the REST approach facilitates the development of client applications and application components for specialized needs. Implementing a RESTful client requires very little overhead, which is favorable in resource constrained environments such as mobile devices [11,13]. In addition to easing development of the 10Green mobile app, this design also makes it easy for developers not familiar with the main 10Green code-base to incorporate some of the underlying data, metrics, maps, and other items in their own applications.

2.2   Application Programming Interface (API)

In order to request data from the server, a client interacts with one of the available resources that are published by the server using a set of global identifiers (HTTP URIs). For example, the client may retrieve information about the 10Green carbon monoxide parameter using an HTTP GET request for the URI `http://www.10green.org/api/parameters/co`. The 10Green API transfers the requested resources in a structure that facilitates programmatic access. The two representations currently supported are JSON (JavaScript Object Notation) [5] and XML (Extensible Markup Language) [3]. The API imposes no usage patterns beyond the REST principles and so allows flexible and creative uses of the underlying data, metrics, and map features.

Figure 3 illustrates an example scenario of exploring the 10Green score for Orono, ME. First, the app sends a request to the location resource to retrieve the set of locations matching the user-supplied search criteria of "orono". After the user disambiguates "Orono, ME" from a list of choices, the app requests the score for this location and renders the score summary display (see Fig. 1 above). The score object contains a description of the score as well as the information about the subscores, allowing the user to browse this information without requiring any requests to the server. Finally, if the user requests to view the map for a subscore, the app will request the set of possible rendering options and begin fetching map tiles to render the initial map display.

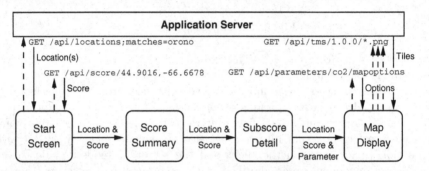

Fig. 3. Client-server interactions utilizing the API

2.3   Tile Mapping Service (TMS)

A TMS is a standard interface [10] to maps of geo-referenced data. Each *map* served by a TMS is composed of a rectangular grid of square *tiles*. The scale of a map is determined by a nonnegative integer called its *zoom level*. A map at zoom level 0 covers the entire globe using only two tiles. Each subsequent zoom level quadruples the number of tiles covering the globe. In general, a complete map at zoom level n is a rectangular grid of 2^{2n+1} tiles arranged in 2^n rows and 2^{n+1} columns.

Figure 4 shows an example map that is a composite of tiles made available by the TMS. It illustrates the maximum large particulate readings in the Northeast U.S. compared to the 10Green health standard. The complete map consists of two *layers*: a base layer with geological boundaries and a layer that visualizes a dataset using point graphics. An example tile from each layer is shown to the right in the figure.

The TMS employed in the 10Green API is designed to be able to efficiently and dynamically serve a very large number (potentially unlimited) of unique tiles that would be infeasible or impossible to completely pre-render and host. Consider a 33 gigabyte dataset that consists of 32 years of hourly measurements of ten pollutants for the United States. If the TMS is configured to generate hourly plots (280,512) for these pollutants using ten possible zoom levels (699,050 total

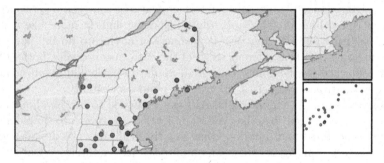

Fig. 4. A composite map, base layer tile, and dataset tile

tiles per map) and one fixed set of parameters for *how* the data is visualized, then there are roughly 2×10^{12} possible tiles. Assuming that the average size of a tile is 500 bytes (for point datasets many of the tiles will be very sparse or empty, especially at higher zoom levels), the complete size of the tile space is approximately 9×10^{14} bytes. The time that it would take to pre-generate these tiles, and the costs associated with hosting this amount of data, are prohibitive for projects with modest budgets.

By supporting on-demand generation of tiles, the TMS greatly reduces the amount of static storage space required to deploy the application, which increases the options for deployment and minimizes cloud storage costs (at the expense of slightly more computationally expensive requests). An experiment was performed to compare the total transfer times between dynamically generated and static tiles, where the tiles from the first six zoom levels were requested for each of the tile sets. Transfer time for the static tile set averaged 0.182s (0.039s standard deviation; 0.543s max), while dynamically-generated large particulates and sulfur dioxide averaged 0.189s (0.094s SD; 3.245s max) and 0.187s (0.187s SD; 0.740s max), respectively. These results show that, on average, the generation time is eclipsed by transmission time. The exceptions are the tiles at the lowest zoom levels for large datasets, which could benefit from pre-generation or caching priority. When requesting a map from the server, clients will often request tens or hundreds of tiles in a short period of time. The 10Green server design, based on REST principles, ensures that a client can use any of the available servers. (See Sect. 3.)

2.4 Mobile App Development

An early version of the 10Green app simply downloaded and displayed a simplified version of the 10Green Web application based on mobile Web standards. This is an attractive and popular approach to application development, as it requires very little device-specific code and can be quickly ported to many mobile platforms. However, this approach yielded an application that was sluggish, didn't implement the standard interface conventions, and required full page refreshes every time a page option was changed or the user navigated between views of the data. A second version of the app utilized the same mobile Web approach but included some native interface features that could be controlled via JavaScript callbacks. This app, while behaving slightly more like a native application, still suffered from the sluggishness of having to do full page loads while navigating between different views of the data. Additionally, both of these approaches lacked the flexibility that good applications should exhibit, such as supporting multiple screen sizes, orientations, and accessibility.

To solve these issues, the RESTful API was extended to expose all of the important resources used by the Web application in order to implement a convenient and functional interface that greatly facilitates the design and implementation of applications that can employ the native interface features and conventions. Mobile applications can take advantage of the API to implement an efficient and cohesive experience. Users can navigate between different views of the same data (such as the parameters that contribute to a score) without requiring full page loads from a Web server, since the complete information of what constitutes the score can be downloaded to the device in a single transaction. While this method for application development requires significantly more native code, the code necessary to implement a REST client is minimal. As opposed to a strategy to replicate the same (or functionally similar) interfaces on multiple devices (e.g., [9] [1]), this approach grants developers more freedom in how they can utilize and interact with the underlying dataset, at the cost of a loss of homogeneity between applications.

3   Cloud Deployment

This section describes the design decisions for the 10Green application server's data-access architecture and provisioning on a cloud infrastructure, followed by a few experimental highlights.

3.1   Database Access

When transitioning from single to multiple server instances, we identified two main schemes for the deployment of the application server based on the database access modes: *shared-nothing* and *shared-database*. In the shared-nothing scheme, the application database is replicated on all virtual instances of the application server. In the shared-database scheme, all instances of the application server share a single instance of the database running on a dedicated database server instance.

Scalability is greatly increased at the expense of write complexity in the shared-nothing scheme. For read-only datasets, or datasets that are only infrequently updated, this deployment scheme is very efficient. As load increases, additional server instances can be added easily without any coordination with existing instances. A requirement of this approach is a mechanism for keeping the dataset on the server instances up to date. This requirement is trivially satisfied by applications with read-only datasets. For many other applications, a simple option is redeploying new server disk images with the updated dataset.

This option benefits from the ability to deploy new instances, and remove old ones, efficiently. Another option is shipping database update transactions to the existing server instances, each of which updates its database locally. Such a solution requires the application semantics to be tolerant of short-term differences in the databases on different server instances. For applications with stricter requirements on update semantics, a more sophisticated database update scheme, or the shared-database scheme, must be used.

In the shared-database scheme, database updates and consistency are easily achieved using standard database methods since all application server instances use the same database instance. Further, since the database is instantiated only once, this scheme is well suited to applications with databases whose size would impose excessive requirements if replicated in each application server instance. Like the shared-nothing scheme above, this scheme also allows for efficient and lightweight addition and removal of server instances in order to adapt to varying load conditions. Modifying an application server from the shared-nothing scheme to the shared-database scheme is trivial, typically requiring only a small change in the configuration for the database connection pool to connect to the external database rather than a local one. An obvious disadvantage of the shared-database scheme is that the database is a potential performance bottleneck since it must handle requests from all application server instances. The potential for this bottleneck can be minimized by using a server that is capable of handling the number of connections for the estimated number of application server instances in a highest-use scenario, or the fixed maximum number of instances when set in a deployment configuration. Another disadvantage of this scheme is that the dedicated database server can significantly increase the minimum cost of deployment.

Both of these deployment schemes benefit from the RESTful design of the application server's interfaces. It is popular to use HTTP *sessions*, an association of information with individual clients, to track the state of the client-server interaction. In many implementations, session support is partially implemented using *server affinity*: clients are assigned to one server for the duration of that session. The unfortunate downside to server affinity is that clients that have been assigned to an overloaded server during an automatic scaling operation will not be reassigned to new server instances. The older, overloaded instances will retain their heavy load while new instances will be under-utilized, partially negating the benefits of the automatic scaling. (See Sect. 3.3.)

The initial deployment of the 10Green application uses the shared-nothing scheme. An important feature permitting this choice is that 10Green datasets are read-only from the client side. The datasets are updated only infrequently when new information is available and assimilated from the various underlying sources of data; the expected update frequency is monthly or weekly at most. Further, although the 10Green database in its initial form is too large to deploy to multiple application server instances, we are able to redesign the application to use the much smaller aggregate datasets to overcome this hurdle.

3.2   Server Instance Provisioning

The 10Green application uses *Amazon Web Services (AWS)* [2] as the deployment platform due to its reported reliability and pay-for-what-you-use pricing. An important decision in such deployments is the choice of server instance types from the options offered by the provider. The two AWS instance types most suited to this application are the low-cost "micro" ($0.02 per hour) and "small" ($0.06 per hour) types. The small instance type has 1.7 GiB of memory and a dedicated compute unit, while the micro instance has 613 MiB of memory and a variable-rate compute unit that can throttle to two units for brief periods of time.[2] In the case of the micro unit, the variable-rate computing unit is designed for processing loads that are normally relatively low, such as serving Web pages, with periodic spikes, such as rendering a TMS image that consists of many data points. The main shortcoming of the micro instance type is the lack of instance storage (the small type offers 160 GB), which is needed for a per-instance file cache for generated images. Because a large number of the files that can be requested by the user are created dynamically, the use of a local cache and a standard caching strategy could greatly increase the average response time of the application server.

3.3   Experimental Highlights

This section presents brief highlights of our preliminary experimental study of the cloud deployment. The server deployments were configured using Elastic Beanstalk deployments with a > 50% CPU utilization trigger for adding instances and a < 20% trigger for removing instances. Unless otherwise specified, the small instance type and one initial instance was used for these experiments. Request load was generated using a variable-sized client pool that continuously requested dynamically generated images from the TMS. Tiles were requested from the large particulates dataset by sequentially varying the $y-$ and $x-$axes, the zoom (0-6), and the year (the last 30 years).

Session Affinity. Figure 5 summarizes the results of a simple experiment using a pool of 20 session-aware clients that demonstrates the penalty that session affinity effects on performance in a parallel environment. The first scaling operation finished at approximately five minutes into each test; however, in the case of the server using session affinity, none of the new servers were utilized. Notice that shortly after the first scaling operation, the plots diverge significantly. The server with affinity continues to be able to process under 2,000 requests per minute, while the other server can benefit from the redistribution of load onto the new servers to greatly increase the rate at which it can process incoming requests. The server with no affinity later benefited from a second scaling operation while the other continued to service requests using the original instance, as none of the aggregate metrics were high enough to trigger a second scaling event.

---

[2] An EC2 compute unit is approximately equivalent to a 1.0 GHz 2007 Xeon processor.

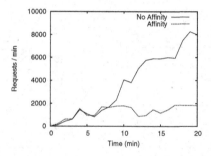

Fig. 5. Impact of session affinity on performance

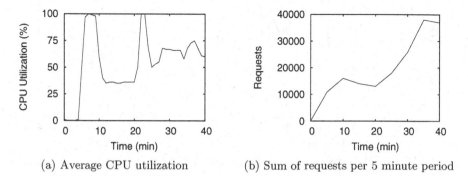

(a) Average CPU utilization   (b) Sum of requests per 5 minute period

Fig. 6. Experimental results of scaling operation using the small instance type

Autoscaling Tests. The initial 10Green experimental deployments used the micro instance because of its low cost. Utilizing many available servers, even with modest memory and processing speed, is well suited in particular for the tile mapping system where many tiles may be requested by the same client. For these tests a variable number of client instances were used (5 initially, 5 added every five minutes to a maximum of 25), caching was disabled, and the scaling increment was two new server instances.

The first experiment, using a micro instance type, resulted in an almost instant failure of the application. Even though the framework noticed the increase in load and spawned additional instances, the limited I/O performance of the micro instance was a major bottleneck, causing the application to be unavailable.

The experiment with the small instance, on the other hand, yielded a deployment that scaled successfully. In particular, it demonstrated an ability to manage significant spikes in usage, with very limited periods of high latency. Some results of this experiment are summarized in Fig. 6. As the rate of requests increased (Fig. 6b), the average CPU utilization (Fig. 6a) crosses the 50% threshold and causes two new instances of the application server to be spawned, which in turn causes a drastic decrease in the utilization. Another CPU usage peak occurs as the number of requests climbs even further, but is quickly reduced by the instantiation of another pair of server instances.

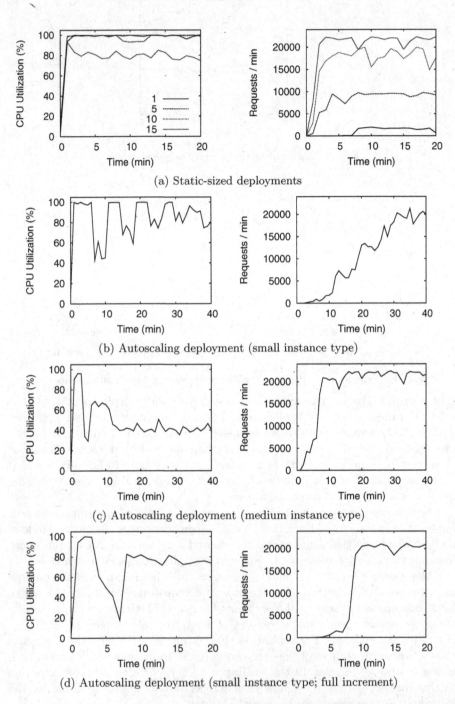

(a) Static-sized deployments

(b) Autoscaling deployment (small instance type)

(c) Autoscaling deployment (medium instance type)

(d) Autoscaling deployment (small instance type; full increment)

Fig. 7. Comparison between static-sized and autoscaling deployments

Static-Sized vs. Autoscaling Deployments. The plots in Fig. 7 illustrate the results of a comparison between several fixed-sized deployments (Fig. 7a) and several autoscaling deployments servicing the requests from 40 client processes (Figs. 7b, 7c, 7d). In Fig. 7b, an autoscaling deployment using a small instance type and a 3-instance scaling increment was used. These results show that one instance is capable of handling just under 2,000 requests per minute, and doubling the number of instances doubles the number of requests that can be processed. Only the 15 instance deployment is capable of handling the generated requests without full CPU utilization. The autoscaling deployment, as expected, operates initially like the 1-instance deployment, but as new instances are added (at eight minute intervals to 13 total instances), the number of requests that it can handle per minute quickly improves.

Figure 7c shows the same experiment using a medium instance type which has twice the computational power, and cost, of the small instance type. When fully scaled to match the load (13–15 instances for small; 7 instances for medium), both deployments can successfully process the incoming requests at roughly the same cost per hour. The one benefit of utilizing the larger instance type is that scaling to manage the load finishes much sooner; however, this doubles the base cost of deployment and the same result can be achieved by using a larger scaling increment. For example, the scaling speed the small type deployment can be increased by doubling the scaling increment used. Fig. 7d illustrates the effect of a larger scaling increment, where the deployment immediately scales to the maximum size when it detects a sharp increase in load, but then slowly reduces the number of instances to match the level of demand.

4   Conclusion

We have presented the design, implementation, and deployment of a flexible data-driven application server that supports both Web browser and programmatic interfaces. We have described the benefits of a REST-based design of the client-server interactions that supports efficient and adaptive use of the data by client applications. We compared two deployment strategies, shared-nothing and shared-database, based on database access modes, and presented decision criteria based on the properties of the target application.

A RESTful approach allows for the extreme scalability of the shared-nothing deployment strategy. As each independent application server instance can completely handle any request from any client, any number of instances can be utilized, and the number can be effectively be scaled up or down as the load on the system evolves. Even when the constraints of the application favor the shared-database deployment strategy (prohibitively large, client-writable, or constantly updating), individual clients can still benefit from the parallelism supported by multiple instances of the application server. Each end-user action typically results in tens of requests sent to the application for documents and images, and each of these requests can be serviced in parallel by any or all of the available instances.

The highlights of our experimental study demonstrate the scalability of our approach. In particular, they demonstrate that using a method for maintaining instance independence is important for effectively using a cloud environment. Alternate designs that maintain session state at the server are unable to effectively use dynamic scaling of servers, especially as the length of sessions increases. The experimental study also indicates that our design allows the effective use of inexpensive instance types (from a cloud provider) to provide good price/performance properties without sacrificing responsiveness or throughput.

Acknowledgments. The authors thank all 10Green project members for their contributions. This work was supported in part by the U.S. National Science Foundation grant EAR-1027960, the University of Maine, Garrand, and the Heinz Endowments.

References

1. Hinz, M., Fiala, Z., Wehner, F.: Personalization-based optimization of web interfaces for mobile devices. In: Brewster, S., Dunlop, M.D. (eds.) Mobile HCI 2004. LNCS, vol. 3160, pp. 204–215. Springer, Heidelberg (2004)
2. Amazon elastic compute cloud (April 2013), http://aws.amazon.com/ec2/
3. Bray, T., Paoli, J., Sperberg-McQueen, C.M., Maler, E., Yergeau, F.: Extensible markup language (xml) 1.0 (fifth edition). World Wide Web Consortium, Recommendation REC-xml-20081126 (November 2008)
4. Chen, C., Chen, G., Jiang, D., Ooi, B.C., Vo, H.T., Wu, S., Xu, Q.: Providing scalable database services on the cloud. In: Chen, L., Triantafillou, P., Suel, T. (eds.) WISE 2010. LNCS, vol. 6488, pp. 1–19. Springer, Heidelberg (2010)
5. Crockford, D.: The application/json media type for JavaScript object notation (JSON). IETF Network Working Group. Request for Comments 4627 (July 2006), http://www.ietf.org/
6. Curino, C., Jones, E., Popa, R.A., Malviya, N., Wu, E., Madden, S., Balakrishnan, H., Zeldovich, N.: Relational Cloud: A Database Service for the Cloud. In: 5th Biennial Conference on Innovative Data Systems Research, Asilomar, CA (January 2011)
7. Fielding, R.: Architectural Styles and the Design of Network-based Software Architectures. Ph.D. thesis, University of California, Irvine (2000)
8. Fielding, R.T., Taylor, R.N.: Principled design of the modern Web architecture. ACM Transactions on Internet Technology 2(2), 115–150 (2002)
9. de Oliveira, R., da Rocha, H.V.: Towards an approach for multi-device interface design. In: Proceedings of the 11th Brazilian Symposium on Multimedia and the Web, WebMedia 2005, pp. 1–3 (2005)
10. Open Source Geospatial Foundation: Tile Map Service specification version 1.0 (April 2011), http://wiki.osgeo.org/
11. Taherkordi, A., Eliassen, F., Romero, D., Rouvoy, R.: RESTful Service Development for Resource-constrained Environments. In: Wilde, E., Pautasso, C. (eds.) REST: From Research to Practice, pp. 221–236. Springer (2011)
12. Wilde, E., Pautasso, C. (eds.): REST: From Research to Practice. Springer (2011)
13. Yazar, D., Dunkels, A.: Efficient application integration in IP-based sensor networks, p. 43. ACM Press (2009)

Using Multiple Data Stores in the Cloud: Challenges and Solutions

Rami Sellami and Bruno Defude

Institut TELECOM, CNRS UMR Samovar, Evry, France
{rami.sellami,bruno.defude}@telecom-sudparis.eu

Abstract. Cloud computing has recently emerged as a new computing paradigm. This latter provides provisioning of dynamically scalable and often virtualized resources which are offered as services. In this context, there is a services pool that supports platforms and mechanisms in order to guarantee the applications development and execution. This set of services is called platform as a service (PaaS). One of the main goals of the PaaS is to support large data stores by ensuring elasticity, scalability and portability. Many applications have to manage different types of data that a single store can not efficiently support. Consequently, clouds need to deploy multiple data stores, allowing applications to choose those corresponding to their data requirements. In this paper, we present and discuss the requirements of such environments and analyze current state of the art.

Keywords: Large data store, Cloud computing, Polyglot persistence, Data management contract, PaaS, Data mediation, Data consistency.

1 Introduction

Cloud computing, a relatively recent term, has become nowadays a buzzword in the Web applications world. Despite the importance of this paradigm, there is no consensus on the cloud computing definition. In this context, experts present a set of twenty one definitions of cloud computing [1]. Based on these definitions, we can define cloud computing as a large scale distributed computing paradigm based on virtualized computing and storage resources, and modern Web technologies. Over the internet network, cloud computing provides scalable and abstracted resources as services. All these services are on demand and offered on a pay-per-use model.

Cloud computing is often presented at three levels: Infrastructure as a Service (IaaS) where clients can deploy their own software, Platform-as-a-Service (PaaS) where clients can program their own applications using the services of the PaaS and finally Sofwtare as a Service (SaaS) where clients use existing applications of the cloud. In this paper, we focus on the PaaS level. Several PaaS commercial solutions exist (e.g. Microsoft Azure [2], Salesforce Force.com [3], Google App Engine [4], etc.) and many research projects are seeking to improve the security, scalability, elasticity and interoperability in the PaaS.

A. Hameurlain, W. Rahayu, and D. Taniar (Eds.): Globe 2013, LNCS 8059, pp. 87–98, 2013.
© Springer-Verlag Berlin Heidelberg 2013

Some researches, Bigtable [5], PNUTS [6], Dynamo [7], etc., take into account the data management in the cloud. Nevertheless, they are not sufficient to address all the goals of data management in the PaaS which are [8]: (i) designing scalable database management architectures, (ii) enabling elasticity and less complexity during databases migration, and (iii) designing intelligent and autonomic DBMS. Indeed, an application uses in most cases a single Data Base Management System (DBMS or data store) to manage its data. This DBMS is supposed to support the whole needs of an application. Thus, it seems illusory to find a single DBMS that efficiently supports various applications with different requirements in terms of data management.

We focus, in this paper, on existing solutions of the state-of-the-art supporting multiple data stores in the cloud. More precisely, our contributions are (i) describe different scenarios related to the way applications use data stores in a PaaS (ii) define the data requirements of applications in a PaaS (iii) analyze and classify existing works on cloud data management, focusing on multiple data stores requirements.

The rest of this paper is organized as follows. Section 2 presents three scenarios in order to define the application requirements in term of cloud data storage. In sections 3 and 4, we analyze the state of the art related to these requirements. In Section 5, we present a synthesis of this analysis. Section 6 provides a conclusion and some open issues.

2   Data Storage Requirements in the Cloud

Different forms of interaction between applications and DBMSs (or data stores) are possible in a cloud environment. In order to define the application requirements in term of data storage, we analyze three possible scenarios (see Fig.1). Regardless the scenario, applications are deployed in the cloud because they require scalability and elasticity. These properties will interact with other requirements and mainly with the requirements related to consistency. The first requirement is:

– R_0: Ensuring scalability and elasticity.

In the first scenario S_1 one or more applications use the same cloud data store. Indeed, the cloud provider provides just one data store for cloud applications. In Fig.1, this scenario is depicted by continuous lines. So, implementing an application in such case will be simple and convenient since we will find an unique API to manage the data store. However, it is difficult to a single data store in one cloud to support the needs of all applications. Furthermore, some clients will be obliged to migrate their applications in another cloud in order to meet their data requirements.

The second scenario S_2 corresponds to clouds providing multiple data stores. Each client can choose its appropriate data store according to his application needs. This scenario is depicted in Fig.1 by the dashed lines. In addition, due to these multiple data stores, clients are not obliged to migrate to another cloud.

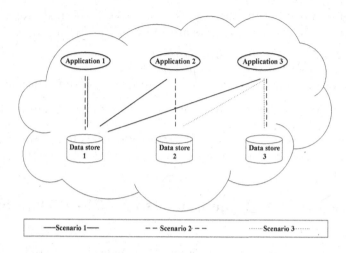

Fig. 1. The three possible scenarios

However, a single application can use only one data store to store all its data. So in some cases, an application may want to migrate its data from one data store (i.g. a relational DBMS) to another (i.g. a NoSQL DBMS). The problem here is to decide if a data store is convenient for an application and if not how to efficiently migrate data from one DBMS to another. Added to the requirement R_0, we identify two new data requirements:

- R_1: Choosing a data store based on data requirements. In this context, we present three sub-requirements: (R_{11}) defining application needs and requirements towards data, (R_{12}) defining data store capabilities, and (R_{13}) defining a matching between application needs and data stores capabilities.
- R_2: Migrating application from a data store to another (i.e. migrating data and adapting the application source code to a new API).

In the third scenario S_3 an application can use multiple data stores. For instance, an application can use a relational data store and a NoSQL data store at the same time or partition its data into multiple data stores. This scenario is illustrated by the dotted lines in Fig.1. Moreover, these data stores may belong to different clouds (e.g. a public cloud and a private one). This ensures a high level of efficiency and modularity. This case corresponds to what is popularly referred to as the polyglot persistence. Nevertheless, this scenario represents some limits and difficulties. Linking an application with multiple data stores is very complex due to the different APIs, data models, query languages or consistency models. If the application needs to query data coming from different data sources (e.g joining data, aggregating data, etc.), it can not do it declaratively unless some kinds of mediation have been done before. Finally, the different data stores may use different transaction and consistency models (for example classical ACID and eventual consistency). It is not easy for programmers to understand these models and to properly code their application to ensure desired properties. For this scenario, three new requirements are added to R_0, R_1, and R_2:

- R_3: Easy access to multiple data stores.
- R_4: Transparent access to integrated data stores.
- R_5: Easy programming of consistency guaranties with different data stores.

In the rest of the paper, we analyze current state of the art regarding these six requirements. We organize this analysis in two parts: the first one deals with requirements concerning the capture of data requirements from applications and the capabilities of data stores. The second part deals with multiple data stores requirements.

3 Capturing Data Requirements and Cloud Data Store Capabilities

In this section, we analyze the requirement R_1. Indeed, we intend to allow an application to bind to one or multiple data stores. For this purpose, we present and discuss some previous works that provide the requirements R_{11}, R_{12}, and R_{13}. We introduce first of all the CAMP standard in order to discover the application needs and the data stores requirements (see Section 3.1). Then, we give a short overview of the CDMI standard that allow to describe and discover data storage capabilities (see Section 3.2). Finally, we discuss works that enable an application to negotiate its requirements with cloud data stores and to express these requirements in data contracts(see Section 3.3). This latter is an agreement between the application and the cloud data stores.

3.1   Cloud Application Management for Platforms (CAMP)

Cloud application management for platforms (CAMP) [9] is a specification defined for applications management, including packaging and deployment, in the PaaS. Indeed, CAMP provides to the application developers a set of interfaces and artifacts based on the REST architecture in order to manage the application deployment and their use of the PaaS resources. An application may be thereafter deployed, run, stopped, suspend, snapshotted, and patched in the PaaS. Concerning the relationship data storage/application, CAMP allows an application to define its needs especially in term of data storage.

CAMP proposes a PaaS resource model. This model allows the developer to control the whole life cycle of his application and its deployment environment. This model contains the four following resources:

- *Platform*: This resource provides an overview on the PaaS and allows to discover which application is running. Indeed, this resource references the deployed applications, the running applications and the PaaS capabilities which are called respectively *Assembly Templates*, *Assemblies*, and *Components*. It also enables the PaaS *capabilities and requirements* discovery. In our case it allows to get a primary view on the application and the data storage platform.

- *Assemblies*: This resource exists under two possible forms. The first one is the *Assembly Template* and it defines a deployed application and its dependencies. Whereas, the second is the *Assembly* and it represents an application instance.
- *Components*: This resource may exist in two kinds that are *Application Component* and *Platform Component*. Each kind may be under two forms also. On the one hand, the *Application Component* and *Application Component Template* define respectively an instantiated instance of an application component and a discrete configuration of a deployed application component. On the other hand, we have *Platform Component* and *Platform Component Template* that represent an instantiated instance of a platform component and a discrete configuration of a platform component.
- *Capabilities and Requirements*: A capability defines the configuration of *Application Components* or *Platform Components*. Whereas a requirement expresses the dependency of an application on an *Application Component* or *Platform Component* and it is created by the application developer or administrator.

As we see through the PaaS resource model of CAMP, there are various resources that are focusing on defining the capabilities of either application or data storage platform. These resources are *Platform, Assembly Template, Application Component Template, Platform Component Template*, and *Capabilities and Requirements*. Hence, it enables the discovery and the publication of application needs in term of data storage that is the requirement R_{11}. Moreover, it allows to define the data stores capabilities which is the requirement R_{12}.

3.2   Cloud Data Management Interface (CDMI)

The Storage Networking Industry Association (SNIA), an association of producers and consumers of storage networking products, has defined a standard for Infrastructure as a Service (IaaS) in the cloud. This standard is referred to as Cloud Data Management Interface (CDMI) [10]. Based on the REST architecture, CDMI allows to create, retrieve, update, and delete data in the cloud. It provides an object model in which the root element is called *Root Container*. This latter represents the main container that will contain all the needed data by an application. This element is related to the following elements:

- *Container*: The *Root Container* element may contain zero or more sub-containers. Each container is characterized by a set of capabilities that will be inherited by the data objects that it contains.
- *Data object*: Each *container* may store zero or more *data objects*. These are used to store data based on the *container* capabilities.
- *Queue object*: The *Queue objects* stores zero or more values. These values are created and fetched in a first-in first-out manner. The queue mechanism organize the data access by allowing one or more writers to send data to a single reader in a reliable way.

- *Domain object*: This element allows to associate the client's ownership with stored objects.
- *Capability object*: The *capability objects* describe the *container*'s capabilities in order to discover the cloud capabilities in term of data storage.

This international standard support several features. Indeed, it enables the available capabilities discovery in the cloud storage offering. In addition, it supports the containers and their contents management. It defines also meta-data to be associated with containers and the objects they contain. So, CDMI allows to define the data stores requirements which is R_{12} but at a lower level (it is more infrastructure oriented than platform oriented).

3.3   Data Management Contract

Truong et al. [11,12,13] propose to model and specify data concerns in data contracts to support concern-aware data selection and utilization in 'Service as a Service (SaaS). For this purpose, they define an abstract model to specify a data contract using terms such as data rights, pricing model, etc. Moreover, they propose some algorithms and techniques in order to enforce the data contract usage. In fact, they present a data contract compatibility evaluation algorithm. This latter allows the combination of multiple data assets (Data mashup). In addition, they introduce a model (called DEscription MOdel for DaaS or DEMODS [12]) for exchanging data agreements based on a new type of services which is referred to as Data Agreement Exchange as a Service (DAES) [11]. However, Truong et al. propose this data contract for service selection and composition and not to store data or to help the developer to choose the appropriate data stores for his application.

Ruiz-Alvarez et al. [14] propose an automated approach to select the PaaS storage services according to a given application requirements. For this purpose, they define an XML schema based on a machine readable description of the capabilities of each storage system. This XML schema allows consumers to express their storage needs using high-level concepts. In addition, it is used to match consumer's requirements and the data storage capabilities.

In summary, the current works on Data Management Contracts (DMCs), often referred to as data agreements or data licenses, are not tailored to our purpose which is to allow an application to bind to the appropriate data stores according to its requirements. A possible solution is to use DMC to implement the data storage offerings and the application needs matching that is the requirement R_{13}. CDMI and CAMP are interesting inputs in this direction.

4   Multiple Data Stores Requirements

In this section we analyze the requirements associated to the multiple data stores scenario S_3 and describe the state of the art. It corresponds to the polyglot persistence case [15]. Three requirements have been identified: (R_3) the application wants to query different data stores in an easy way that is without having to deal with the DBMS proprietary APIs (Section 4.1), (R_4) the application wants to transparently access to the different data stores and to issue queries on several data sources (Section 4.2), and (R_5) application consistency and its relationship with scalability and elasticity (Section 4.3).

4.1 Easy Access to Multiple Data Stores

In some cases, applications want to store and manipulate explicitly their data in multiple data stores. Applications know in advance the set of data stores to use and how to distribute their data on these stores. However, in order to simplify the development process, application developers do not want to manipulate different proprietary APIs. Furthermore, it is impossible to write queries manipulating data coming from different data stores (such as a join between two data stores).

Two classes of solutions can be used in this case. The first one is based on the definition of a neutral API capable to support access to the different data stores. In the context of relational DBMSs, there are several ones such as JDBC for Java applications. It is more complex in the cloud's context because there are a large number of possible data stores, which are quite heterogeneous in all dimensions: data model, query language, transaction model, etc. In particular, NoSQL DBMSs are widely used in cloud environment and are not standard at all: their data model are different (key/value, document, graph or column-oriented), their query languages are proprietary and they implement consistency models based on eventual consistency.

It is therefore difficult to define such a generic API but several efforts have been made. The Spring Data Framework [16] is an attempt in this direction and offers some generic abstractions to handle different types of NoSQL DBMSs. These abstractions are refined for each DBMS. The addition of a new data store is not so easy and the solution is strongly linked to the Java programming model.

The second class is based on the model-driven architecture and engineering methodology [17]. An abstract model of applications, including data store accesses, is defined and automatically transformed into a concrete model (linked to a specific data store) through transformations. At the end this concrete model is transformed into a set of programming statements. The main problem here, is to define such an abstract model due to the large heterogeneity of target data stores. Some preliminary works have proposed to use such an approach ([18] for example) but no complete proposals have been made for the moment.

[19] propose another approach to this problem. They define the new notion of DBMS+ which is a DBMS encapsulating different execution and storage engines. Applications issue queries against the DBMS+ together with data requirements for the application (latency bounds, desired recovery time under faults, etc.). The DBMS+ optimizer analyzes these inputs and produces an optimized execution plan including the choice of the best execution and storage engine. This approach supposes that data can be easily moved from one storage system to another but there are some interesting initiatives of neutral serialization formats such as protocol-buffers [20].

[21] is based on the ideas coming from extensible DBMS, adopted to scalability and elasticity needed by cloud environments. They propose Cloudy a modular cloud storage system, based on a generic data model, and which can be customized to meet application requirements. Cloudy offers to an application several external interfaces (key/value, SQL, XQuery, etc.) while supporting different storage engines (such as BerkeleyDB or in-memory hash-map). Each Cloudy node in the system is a autonomous running process executing the entire Cloudy stack. Cloudy supports several replication and partitioning schemes for distributing the load across nodes. The main problem with such approaches is that the addition or modification of components requires high specialist and even programmers need to be aware of many technical details to master this type of platform.

4.2 Transparent Access to Integrated Data Stores

It is a classical problem which has been widely addressed by the data mediation community [22]. Two types of components are used to allow different data sources to be integrated and manipulated in a transparent way: a mediator and adapters. The mediator hides the sources to applications. It implements a global schema described in a neutral data model and including all the information to share. There are two approaches to design the schema, global-as-view (the global schema is defined as a view on the data sources) and local-as-view (the data sources are defined as views on the predefined global schema). Applications issue queries on the global schema using the query language associated to the neutral data model and the mediator rewrite these queries as sub-queries send to the target data sources. Each data source is encapsulated by an adapter transforming a neutral query into a (set of) data source query.

In our context, this approach is not so easy because of the important heterogeneity of the data stores, especially related to their data models and query languages. [23] is a first attempt in this direction. It proposes a mediation system aiming at supporting document and column family data stores. The relational data model is used to define the global schema whereas NoSQL and relational DBMSs are target data sources. A mapping language has been proposed to map attributes of the data sources to the global schema. The mapping language supports different access paths to the same relation as well as multi-valued or nested attributes. Query rewriting is done using a bridge query language allowing to bridge the gap between a declarative language as SQL and the imperative languages implemented by many NoSQL data stores. This proposal is promising even if some functionalities are lacking (no query optimization at the global level for example).

4.3 Consistency, Scalability and Elasticity

Scalability represents a static property that specify the behavior of a system based on a static configuration. Elasticity defines a dynamic property that enables to scale up and down the system on demand, at runtime.

These are fundamental properties in the cloud which have strong relationships with consistency guaranties. In fact, scaling and strong consistency are somewhere antagonist: if you want strong consistency, your system can not scale and if you want system scalability you have to relax consistency or to impose restrictions on your application (for example maintaining transaction's updates within a single data store).

In [8], Agrawal et al. define two manners to ensure scalability. In the one hand, they define the *data fusion* that combined multiple small data granules to provide transactional guarantees when scaling larger data granules. That is the approach of Google's Bigtable [5], Amazon's Dynamo [7] and Yahoo's PNUTS [6]. In the other hand, they present the *data fission* which splits a database into independent shards or partitions and provide transactional guarantees only on these shards (relational cloud [24] and ElasTraS [25]).

Live database migration is a key component to ensure elasticity. In *shared disk architecture* (Bigtable [5] and ElasTraS [25]), you have to migrate the database cache but persistent data are stored in a network attached storage and do not need migration while in *shared nothing disk architecture* (Zephyr [26]) you need also to migrate persistent data which are quite larger than cache data.

Consistency has been widely studied in the context of transactions (see [27] for a general presentation of distributed transaction processing). A strong consistency model has emerged for relational DBMSs named ACID (Atomicity, Consistency, Isolation and Durability). This model is difficult to scale that is the reason why large scale web applications have popularize a new kind of consistency model named the BASE model (Basically Available, Soft state and Eventual consistency). BASE ensures scalability but at the cost of a more complex writing of applications, because programmers have to manually ensure part of the consistency. For example, applications have to access only data in a single node, avoiding the use of costly distributed protocols to synchronize nodes.

Several works try to help programmers in their task. [24] developed a workload-aware partitioner which uses graph-partitioning to analyze complex query workloads and proposes a mapping of data items to node that minimize the number of multi-node transactions/statements. [28] is a recent work addressing the problem of client-centric consistency on top of eventually consistent distributed data stores (Amazon S3 for example). It consists in a middleware service running on the same server than the application and providing the same behavior than a causally consistent data store even in the presence of failures or concurrent updates. This service uses vector clocks and client-side caching to ensure client-centric properties. The main interest of this proposal is that it comes at a low cost and it is transparent for programmers.

[29] presents a new transaction paradigm, where programmers can specify different consistency guaranties at the data level. The system ensures these guaranties and allows for certain data to dynamically switch from one consistency level to another depending on live statistics on data. Three classes of consistency are defined: class A corresponds to serialisable or strong consistency, class B corresponds to session consistency (minimum acceptable level of consistency

for programmers) and class C corresponds to data supporting either class A or class C consistency levels, depending on their actual value. For example, in a product inventory application, if the available stock value is high, it can tolerates a low consistency level but if it is near to a given threshold the strongest consistency level is needed. The main interest of this approach, is that we pay only for the needed consistency level and at a fine granularity level.

5   Synthesis

In Table 1, we present a synthesis of the main works that we have analyzed in previous sections. Even if all requirements are addressed by at least one work, no work addresses all the requirements. In fact, the majority of the works that we presented focused on the requirements R_1 and R_3 which are the *choice of a data store based on data requirements* and the *easy access to integrated data stores*. Less importance is given to the requirements R_0, R_2, and R_5 that are respectively the *scalability and elasticity ensuring*, the *migration of an application from a data store to another*, and the *easy programming of consistency guaranties with different data stores*. Nonetheless, there is just one work that proposes an approach for ensuring the *transparent access to integrated data stores* which represents the requirement R_4.

Table 1. Synthesis of the state-of-the-art

	R_0	R_1	R_2	R_3	R_4	R_5
CDMI [10,30]		R_{11}				
CAMP [9]		$R_{11,12}$				
Data contract [11,12,13,14]		$R_{12,13}$				
Spring Data [16]				x		
MDA/MDE [18]				x		
DBMS+[19]			x	x		
Cloudy [21]				x		
Curé et al. [23]					x	
Relational Cloud [24]	x		x			x
Protocol Buffers [20]			x			
Bermbach et al. [28]						x

This lack of solutions implies that programers need to address most of the requirements by themselves and so they have to be aware of many technical details. More works have to be done to simplify data-intensive application development in the context of PaaS.

6   Conclusion

In this paper, we have defined and classified the applications requirements in term of multiple-data stores in the PaaS through three possible scenarios.

We have analyzed the literature regarding these requirements and presented a synthesis of this analysis. This synthesis shows that many works are still needed to support all desired requirements. We are currently working to address part of these requirements, focusing on the design and implementation of a contract-based approach, allowing applications to negotiate the best data store corresponding to their data requirements.

References

1. Geelan, J., et al.: Twenty-one experts define cloud computing
2. Team, M.: Microsoft azure (2013)
3. Weissman, C.D., Bobrowski, S.: The design of the force.com multitenant internet application development platform. In: Proceedings of the 2009 ACM SIGMOD International Conference on Management of Data, pp. 889–896 (2009)
4. Google: Google appengine documentation (2009)
5. Fay, C., et al.: Bigtable: A distributed storage system for structured data. ACM Trans. Comput. Syst. 26(2) (2008)
6. Cooper, B.F., et al.: Pnuts: Yahoo!'s hosted data serving platform. PVLDB 1(2), 1277–1288 (2008)
7. DeCandia, G.: et al.: Dynamo: amazon's highly available key-value store. In: Proceedings of the 21st ACM Symposium on Operating Systems Principles, SOSP 2007, October 14-17, pp. 205–220. Stevenson, Washington (2007)
8. Agrawal, D., El Abbadi, A., Das, S., Elmore, A.J.: Database scalability, elasticity, and autonomy in the cloud. In: Yu, J.X., Kim, M.H., Unland, R. (eds.) DASFAA 2011, Part I. LNCS, vol. 6587, pp. 2–15. Springer, Heidelberg (2011)
9. Mark, C., et al.: Cloud application management for platforms (August 2012)
10. SNIA: Cloud data management interface (June 2012)
11. Truong, H.L., et al.: Exchanging data agreements in the daas model. In: 2011 IEEE Asia-Pacific Services Computing Conference, APSCC 2011, Jeju, Korea (South), December 12-15, pp. 153–160 (2011)
12. Vu, Q.H.: et al.: Demods: A description model for data-as-a-service. In: IEEE 26th International Conference on Advanced Information Networking and Applications, AINA, Fukuoka, Japan, March 26-29, pp. 605–612 (2012)
13. Truong, H.L., Comerio, M., Paoli, F.D., Gangadharan, G.R., Dustdar, S.: Data contracts for cloud-based data marketplaces. IJCSE 7(4), 280–295 (2012)
14. Ruiz-Alvarez, A., Humphrey, M.: An automated approach to cloud storage service selection. In: Proceedings of the 2nd International Workshop on Scientific Cloud Computing, ScienceCloud 2011, pp. 39–48. ACM, New York (2011)
15. Martin, F.: Polyglot persistence (November 2011)
16. Pollack, M., et al.: Spring Data, vol. 1. O'Reilly Media (October 2012)
17. Poole, J.D.: Model-driven architecture: Vision, standards and emerging technologies. In: ECOOP 2001, Workshop on Metamodeling and Adaptive Object Models (2001)
18. Peidro, J.E., Muñoz-Escoí, F.D.: Towards the next generation of model driven cloud platforms. In: CLOSER 2011 - Proceedings of the 1st International Conference on Cloud Computing and Services Science, Noordwijkerhout, Netherlands, May 7-9, pp. 494–500 (2011)
19. Lim, H., Han, Y., Babu, S.: How to fit when no one size fits. In: CIDR 2013, Sixth Biennial Conference on Innovative Data Systems Research, January 6-9, Online Proceedings, Asilomar, CA (2013)

20. Google: Protocol buffers (2012)
21. Kossmann, D., et al.: Cloudy: A modular cloud storage system. PVLDB 3(2), 1533–1536 (2010)
22. Doan, A., Halevy, A.Y., Ives, Z.G.: Principles of Data Integration, 1st edn. Morgan Kaufmann (2012)
23. Curé, O., Hecht, R., Le Duc, C., Lamolle, M.: Data integration over NoSQL stores using access path based mappings. In: Hameurlain, A., Liddle, S.W., Schewe, K.-D., Zhou, X. (eds.) DEXA 2011, Part I. LNCS, vol. 6860, pp. 481–495. Springer, Heidelberg (2011)
24. Curino, C.: et al.: Relational cloud: a database service for the cloud. In: CIDR 2011, Fifth Biennial Conference on Innovative Data Systems Research, January 9-12, Online Proceedings, pp. 235–240. Asilomar, CA (2011)
25. Das, S., Agrawal, D., El Abbadi, A.: Elastras: An elastic, scalable, and self-managing transactional database for the cloud. ACM Trans. Database Syst. 38(1), 5 (2013)
26. Elmore, A.J., Das, S., Agrawal, D., El Abbadi, A.: Zephyr: live migration in shared nothing databases for elastic cloud platforms. In: Proceedings of the ACM SIG-MOD International Conference on Management of Data, June 12-16, pp. 301–312. Athens, Greece (2011)
27. Oszu, T.M., Valduriez, P.: Principles of Distributed Database Systems, 3rd edn. Springer (2011)
28. Bermbach, D.: et al.: A middleware guaranteeing client-centric consistency on top of eventually consistent datastores. In: First IEEE International Conference on Cloud Engineering, IEEE IC2E 2013, San Francisco, CA, USA, March 25-28 (2013)
29. Kraska, T., Hentschel, M., Alonso, G., Kossmann, D.: Consistency rationing in the cloud: Pay only when it matters. PVLDB 2(1), 253–264 (2009)
30. Livenson, I., Laure, E.: Towards transparent integration of heterogeneous cloud storage platforms. In: Proceedings of the Fourth International Workshop on Data-Intensive Distributed Computing, DIDC 2011, pp. 27–34 (2011)

Repair Time in Distributed Storage Systems*

Frédéric Giroire[1], Şandeep Kumar Gupta[2], Remigiusz Modrzejewski[1],
Julian Monteiro[3], and Stéphane Perennes[1]

[1] Project MASCOTTE, I3S (CNRS/Univ. of Nice)/INRIA, Sophia Antipolis, France
[2] IIT Delhi, New Delhi, India
[3] Department of Computer Science, IME, University of São Paulo, Brazil

Abstract. In this paper, we analyze a highly distributed backup storage system realized by means of nano datacenters (NaDa). NaDa have been recently proposed as a way to mitigate the growing energy, bandwidth and device costs of traditional data centers, following the popularity of cloud computing. These service provider-controlled peer-to-peer systems take advantage of resources already committed to always-on set top boxes, the fact they do not generate heat dissipation costs and their proximity to users.

In this kind of systems redundancy is introduced to preserve the data in case of peer failures or departures. To ensure long-term fault tolerance, the storage system must have a self-repair service that continuously reconstructs the fragments of redundancy that are lost. In the literature, the reconstruction times are modeled as independent. In practice, however, numerous reconstructions start at the same time (when the system detects that a peer has failed).

We propose a new analytical framework that takes into account this correlation when estimating the repair time and the probability of data loss. We show that the load is unbalanced among peers (young peers inherently store less data than the old ones). The models and schemes proposed are validated by mathematical analysis, extensive set of simulations, and experimentation using the GRID5000 test-bed platform. This new model allows system designers to operate a more accurate choice of system parameters in function of their targeted data durability.

1   Introduction

Nano datacenters (NaDa) are highly distributed systems owned and controlled by the service provider. This alleviates the need of incentives and mitigates the risk of malicious users, but otherwise they face the same challenges as peer-to-peer systems. The set-top boxes realizing them are connected using consumer links, which can be relatively slow, unreliable and congested. The devices themselves, compared to servers in a traditional datacenter, are prone to failures and temporary disconnections, e.g. if the user cuts the power supply when not in

---

* The research leading to these results has received funding from the European Project FP7 EULER, ANR CEDRE, ANR AGAPE, Associated Team AlDyNet, project ECOS-Sud Chile and région PACA.

A. Hameurlain, W. Rahayu, and D. Taniar (Eds.): Globe 2013, LNCS 8059, pp. 99–110, 2013.
© Springer-Verlag Berlin Heidelberg 2013

home. When originally proposed in [1], they were assumed to be available no more than 85% of the time, with values as low as 7% possible.

In this paper we concentrate on application of NaDa, or any similar *peer-to-peer* system, for backup storage. In this application, users want to store massive amounts of data indefinitely, accessing them very rarely, i.e. only when original copies are lost. Due to risk of peer failures or departures, redundancy data is introduced to ensure long term data survival. The redundancy needs to be maintained by a self-repair process. Its speed is crucial to determine the system reliability, as long repairs exponentially increase the probability of losing data. The limiting factor, in this setting, is the upload link capacity.

Imagine a scenario where the system is realized using home connections, out of which an average 128kbps are allocated to the backup application. Furthermore, each device is limited to 300GB, while average data stored is 100GB, redundancy is double, 100 devices take part in each repair and the algorithms are as described in the following sections. A naive back-of-envelope computation gives that the time needed to repair contents of a failed device is 17 hours $(= 100 \cdot 8 \cdot 10^6 \text{kb} / (100 \cdot 128 \text{kbps}))$. This translates, by our model, to a probability of data loss per year (PDLPY) of 10^{-8}. But, taking into account all findings presented in this work, the actual time can reach 9 days. This gives a PDLPY of 0.2, many orders of magnitude more than the naive computation. Hence, it is important to have models that estimate accurately the repair time for limited bandwidth.

Our Contribution. We propose a new analytical model that precisely estimates the repair time and the probability of losing data in distributed storage systems. This model takes into account the bandwidth constraints and inherent workload imbalance (young peers inherently store less data than the old ones, thus they contribute asymmetrically to the reconstruction process) effect on the efficiency. It allows system designers to obtain an accurate choice of system parameters to obtain a desired data durability.

We discuss how far the distribution of the reconstruction time given by the model is from the exponential, classically used in the literature. We also show a somewhat counter-intuitive result that we can reduce the reconstruction time by using a less bandwidth efficient Regenerating Code. This is due to a degree of freedom given by erasure codes to choose which peers participate in the repair process.

To the best of our knowledge, this is the first detailed model proposed to estimate the distribution of the reconstruction time under limited bandwidth constraints. We validate our model by an extensive set of simulations and by test-bed experimentation using the GRID'5000 platform[1].

Related Work. Several works related to highly distributed storage systems have been done, and a large number of systems have been proposed [2–4], but few theoretical studies exist. In [5–7] the authors use a Markov chain model to derive the lifetime of the system. In these works, the reconstruction times are independent for each fragment. However, in practice, a large number of repairs start at the same time when a disk is lost, corresponding to tens or hundreds

---

[1] https://www.grid5000.fr/

of GBs of data. Hence, the reconstructions are not independent of each other. Furthermore, in these models, only the average analysis are studied and the impact of congestion is not taken into account.

Dandoush et al. in [8] perform a simulation study of the download and the repairing process. They use the NS2 simulator to measure the distribution of the repair time. They state that a hypo-exponential distribution is a good fit for the block reconstruction time. However, again, concurrent reconstructions are not considered. Picconi et al. in [9] study the durability of storage systems. Using simulations they characterize a function to express the repair rate of systems based on replication. However, they do not study the distribution of the reconstruction time and the case of erasure coding. Venkatesan et al. in [10] study placement strategies for replicated data, deriving a simple approximation for mean time to data loss by studying the expected behaviour of most damaged data block. The closest to our work is [11] by Ford et al., where authors study reliability of distributed storage in Google, what constitutes a datacenter setting. However, they do not look into load imbalance, their model tracks only one *representative* data fragment and is not concerned by competition for bandwidth.

Organization. The remainder of this paper is organized as follows: in the next section we give some details about the studied system. The queuing model is presented in the Section 3. The estimations are then validated via an extensive set of simulations in Section 4. Lastly, in Section 5, we compare the results of the simulations to the ones obtained by experimentation.

2   System Description

This section outlines the mechanisms of the studied system and our modelling assumptions.

Storage. In this work we assume usage of the Regenerating Codes, as described in [12], due to their high storage and bandwidth efficiency. However, the model presented in this paper can be also applied to other redundancy schemes, by a simple adjustment of an overhead factor. More discussion of them follows later in this section. All data stored in the system is divided into *blocks* of uniform size. Each block is further subdivided into s *fragments* of size L_f, with r additional fragments of redundancy. All these $n = s + r$ fragments are distributed among random devices. We assume that in practice this distribution is performed with a Distributed Hash Table overlay like Pastry [13]. This, due to practical reasons, divides devices into subsets called *neighbourhoods* or *leaf sets*.

Our model does not assume ownership of data. The device originally introducing a block into the system is not responsible for its storage or maintenance. We simply deal with a total number of B blocks of data, which results in $F = n \cdot B$ fragments stored in N cooperating devices. As a measure of fairness, or *load balancing*, each device can store up to the same amount of data equal to C fragments. Note that C can not be less than average number of fragments per device $\bar{D} = F/N$.

In the following we treat a device and its disk as synonyms.

Bandwidth. Devices of NaDa are connected using consumer connections. These, in practice, tend to be asymmetric with relatively low upload rates. Furthermore, as the backup application occasionally uploads at maximum throughput for prolonged times, while the consumer expects the application to not interfere with his network usage, we assume it is allocated only a fraction of the actual link capacity. Each device has a maximum upload and download bandwidth, respectively BW_{up} and BW_{down}. We set $BW_{down} = 10BW_{up}$ (in real offerings, this value is often between 4 and 20). The bottleneck of the system is considered to be the access links (e.g. between a DSLAM and an ADSL modem) and not the network internal links.

Availability and Failures. Mirroring requirements of practical systems, we assume devices to stay connected at least a few hours per day. Following the work by Dimakis [12] on network coding, we use values of availability and failure rate from the PlanetLab and Microsoft PCs traces [3]. To distinguish transient unavailability, which for some consumers is expected on a daily basis, from permanent failures, a timeout is introduced. Hence, a device is considered as failed if it leaves the network for more than 24 hours. In that case, all data stored by it is assumed to be lost.

The Mean Time To Failure (MTTF) in the Microsoft PCs and the PlanetLab scenarios are respectively 30 and 60 days. The device failures are then considered as independent, like in [5], and Poissonian with mean value given by the traces explained above. We consider a discrete time in the following and the probability to fail at any given time step is denoted as $\alpha = 1/MTTF$.

Repair Process. When a failure is detected, neighbours of the failed device start a reconstruction process, to maintain desired redundancy level. For each fragment stored at the failed disk, a random device from the neighbourhood is chosen to be the *reconstructor*. It is responsible for downloading necessary data from remaining fragments of the block, reconstructing and storing the fragment.

3   The Queuing Model

We introduce here a *Markov Chain Model* that allows us to estimate the reconstruction time under bandwidth constraints. The model makes an important assumption: the limiting resource is always the upload bandwidth. It is reasonable because download and upload bandwidths are strongly asymmetric in systems built on consumer connections. Using this assumption, we model the storage system with a queue tracking the upload load of the global system.

Model Definition. We model the storage system with a Markovian queuing model storing the upload needs of the global system. The model has one server, Poissonian batch arrivals and deterministic time service ($M^\beta/D/1$, where β is the batch size function). We use a discrete time model, all values are accounted in time steps. The devices in charge of repairs process blocks in a FIFO order.

Chain States. The state of the chain at a time t is the current number of fragments in reconstruction, denoted by $Q(t)$.

Transitions. At each time step, the system reconstructs blocks as fast as its bandwidth allows. The upload bandwidth of the system, $BW_{up}N$, is the limiting resource. Then, the *service* provided by the server is

$$\mu = \rho \frac{BW_{up}N}{L_r},$$

which corresponds to the number of fragments that can be reconstructed at each time step. The factor ρ is the bandwidth efficiency as calculated in the previous section, and L_r is the number of bytes transferred to repair one fragment. Hence, the number of fragments repaired during a time step t is $\mu(t) = \min(\mu, Q(t))$.

The *arrival process* of the model corresponds to device failures. When a failure occurs, all the fragments stored in the failed device are lost. Hence, a large number of block repairs start at the same time. We model this with batch inputs (sometimes also called *bulk arrival* in the literature). The size of an arrival is given by the number of fragments that were stored on the disk.

Disk occupancy follows a truncated geometric distribution. Denote by x the average disk size divided by the average amount of data stored per device. Let ρ be the *factor of efficiency*: the average bandwidth actually used during a repair process divided by the total bandwidth available to all devices taking part in it. It has been observed in simulations that $\rho \approx 1/x$. This has been further confirmed both by experiments and by theoretical analysis, which has to be omitted here due to lack of space, but can be found in the research report [14]. Here we give a brief intuition of the analysis.

First, notice that a new device joins the system empty and is gradually filled throughout its lifetime. Thus, we have disks with heterogeneous occupancy. For $x < 2$ almost all disks in the system are full. Most blocks have a fragment on a full disk. Even for $x = 3$, when only 6% of disks are full, probability of a block having a fragment on a full disk is 92%. Thus the average repair time depends on the time the full disks take, which is in turn x times the average disks take. This shows that load balancing is crucial and for practical systems x should be kept below two.

We define β as a random variable taking values $\beta \in \{0, v, 2v, \ldots, T_{max}v\}$, which represents the number of fragments inside a failed disk Recall that v is the speed at which empty disks get filled, and that $T_{max} = C/v$ is the expected time to fill a disk. Further on, β/v is the expected time to have a disk with β fragments.

The arrival process of the model is Poissonian. A batch arrives during a time step with probability f, with $f \approx \alpha N$. For the simplicity of the exposition, we consider here that only one failure can happen during a time step (note that to ensure this, it is sufficient to choose a small enough time step). Formally, the transitions of the chain are, for $\forall i \geq \mu$,

$$
\begin{array}{lll}
Q_i \to Q_{i-\mu} & \text{with prob. } 1 - f \\
Q_i \to Q_{i-\mu+\beta}, \forall \beta & \text{with prob. } f(1-\alpha)^{\frac{\beta}{v}-1}\alpha \\
Q_i \to Q_{i-\mu+C} & \text{with prob. } f(1 - (1-\alpha)^{T_{max}})
\end{array}
$$

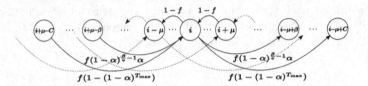

Fig. 1. Transition around state i of the Markovian queuing model

When $0 \leq i < \mu$, the i blocks in the queue at the beginning of the time step are reconstructed at the end. Hence, we have transitions without the term $i - \mu$:

$$Q_i \rightarrow Q_0 \qquad \text{with prob. } 1 - f$$
$$Q_i \rightarrow Q_\beta, \forall \beta \quad \text{with prob. } f(1-\alpha)^{\frac{\beta}{v}-1}\alpha$$
$$Q_i \rightarrow Q_C \qquad \text{with prob. } f(1-(1-\alpha)^{T_{\max}})$$

Figure 1 presents the transitions for a state i.

Analysis. Expressions to estimate the values of the bandwidth usage, the distribution of block reconstruction time and the probability of data loss can be derived from the stationary distribution of the Markovian model. We omit here the analysis due to lack of space, but it can be found in the research report [14].

4   Results

To validate our model, we compare its results with the ones produced by simulations, and test-bed experimentation. We use a custom cycle-based simulator. The simulator models the evolution of the states of blocks during time (number of available fragments and where they are stored) and the reconstructions being processed. When a disk failure occurs, the simulator updates the state of all blocks that have lost a fragment, and starts the reconstruction if necessary. The bandwidth is implemented as a queue for each device, respecting both BW_{up} and BW_{down} constraints. The reconstructions are processed in FIFO order.

We study the distribution of the reconstruction time and compare it with the exponential distribution, which is often used in the literature. We then discuss the cause of the data losses. Finally, we present an important practical implementation point: when choosing the parameters of the Regenerating Code, it is important to *give to the device in charge of the repair a choice between several devices to retrieve the data.*

4.1   Distribution of Reconstruction Time

Figure 2 shows the distribution of the reconstruction time and the impact of device asymmetry on the reconstruction time for the following scenario: N = 100, s = 7, r = 7, L_r=2 MB, B = 50000, MTTF = 60 days, BW_{up} = 128 kpbs. All parameters are kept constant, except the disk size factor x (recall that x is the ratio of the maximum capacity over the average amount of data per device).

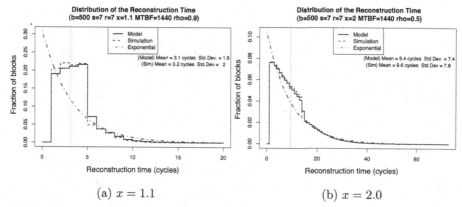

Fig. 2. Distribution of reconstruction time for different disk capacities x of 1.1 and 2 times the average amount. The average reconstruction times of simulations are respectively 3.2 and 9.6 hours (Note that some axis scales are different).

First, we see that the model (dark solid line) closely matches the simulations (blue dashed line). For example, when $x = 1.1$ (left plot), the curves are almost merged. Their shape is explained in the next paragraph, but notice how far they are from the exponential. The average reconstruction times are 3.1 time steps for the model vs 3.2 for the simulation. For $x = 2.0$ (right plot), model is still very close to simulation. However, in this case the exponential is much closer to the obtained shape. In fact, the bigger the value of x, the closer the exponential is. Hence, as we will confirm in the next section, the exponential distribution is only a good choice for some given sets of parameters. Note that the tails of the distributions are close to exponential. Keep in mind that big values of x are impractical due to both storage space and bandwidth inefficiency.

Second, we confirm the strong impact of the disk capacity. We see that for the four considered values of x, the shape of distributions of the reconstruction times are very different. When the disk capacity is close to the average number of fragments stored per disk (values of x close to 1), almost all disks store the same number of fragments (83% of full disks). Hence, each time there is a disk failure in the system, the reconstruction times span between 1 and C/μ, explaining the rectangle shape. The tail is explained by multiple failures happening when the queue is not empty. When x is larger, disks also are larger, explaining that it takes a longer time to reconstruct when there is a disk failure (the average reconstruction time raises from 3.2 to 9.6 and 21 when x raises from 1.1 to 2 and 3).

We ran simulations for different sets of parameters. We present in Table 1 a small subset of these experiments.

4.2 Where the Dead Come from?

In this section, we discuss in which circumstances the system has more probability to lose some data. First a preliminary remark: backup systems are conceived

Table 1. Reconstruction time T (in hours) for different system parameters

	(a) Disk capacity c.				(b) Peer Lifetime (MTTF).				(c) Peer Upload Bandwidth (kbps).			
c	1.1	1.5	2.0	3.0	$MTTF$ 60	120	180	365	$upBW$ 64	128	256	512
T_{sim}	3.26	5.50	9.63	21.12	T_{sim} 3.26	2.90	2.75	2.65	T_{sim} 8.9	3.30	1.70	1.07
T_{model}	3.06	5.34	9.41	21	T_{model} 2.68	2.60	2.49	2.46	T_{model} 8.3	3.10	1.61	1.03

(a) Scenario A   (b) Scenario B

Fig. 3. Distribution of dead blocks reconstruction time for two different scenarios. Scenario A: $N = 200, s = 8, r = 3, b = 1000, MTTF = 60$ days. Scenario B: $N = 200, s = 8, r = 5, b = 2000, MTTF = 90$ days.

to experience basically no data loss. Thus, for realistic sets of parameters, it would be necessary to simulate the system for a prohibitive time to see any data loss. We hence present here results for scenarios where the redundancy of the data is lowered ($r = 3$ and $r = 5$).

In Figure 3 we plot the cumulative number of dead blocks that the system experiences for different reconstruction times. We give the distribution of the reconstruction times as a reference (vertical lines). The model (black solid line) and the simulation results (blue dashed line) are compared for two scenarios with different number of blocks: there is twice more data in Scenario B.

The first observation is that the queuing models predict well the number of dead experienced in the simulation, for example, in the scenario A the values are 21,555 versus 20,879. The results for an exponential reconstruction time with the same mean value are also plotted (queue avg.). We see that this model is not close to the simulation for both scenarios (almost the double for Scenario A). We also test a second exponential model (queue tail): we choose it so that its tail is as close as possible to the tail than the queuing model (see Figures 3b). We see that it gives a perfect estimation of the dead for Scenario B, but not for Scenario A.

In fact, two different phenomena appear in these two scenarios. In Scenario B (higher redundancy), the *lost blocks are mainly coming from long reconstructions*, from 41 to 87 cycles (tail of the gray histogram). Hence, a good exponential model can be found by fitting the parameters to the tail of the queuing model. On the contrary, in Scenario A (lower redundancy), the *data loss comes from*

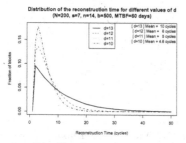

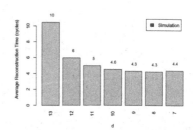

Fig. 4. Distribution of reconstruction time for different values of degree d

Fig. 5. Average Reconstruction Time for different values of degree d. Smaller d implies more data transfers, but may mean smaller reconstruction times!

the majority of short reconstructions, from 5.8 to 16.2 cycles (the right side of the rectangular shape). Hence, in Scenario A, having a good estimate of the tail of the distribution is not at all sufficient to be able to predict the failure rate of the system. It is necessary to have a good model of the complete distribution!

4.3   Discussion of Parameters of Regenerating Codes

As presented in Section 2, when the redundancy is added using regenerating codes, $n = s + r$ devices store a fragment of the block, while just s are enough to retrieve the block. When a fragment is lost d devices, where $s \leq d \leq n - 1$, cooperate to restore it. The larger d is, the smaller is the bandwidth needed for the repair. Figures 4 and 5 show the reconstruction time for different values of the degree d. We observe an interesting phenomena: at the opposite of the common intuition, the average reconstruction time decreases when the degree decreases: 10 cycles for $d = 13$, and only 6 cycles for $d = 12$. The bandwidth usage increases though (because the δ_{MBR} is higher when d is smaller). The explanation is that the decrease of the degree *introduces a degree of freedom* in the choice of devices that send a sub-fragment to the device that will store the repaired fragment. Hence, the system is able to decrease the load of the more loaded disks and to *balance more evenly the load between devices.*

5   Experimentation

Aiming at validating the simulation and the model results, we performed a batch of real experimentation using the GRID'5000 platform. It is an experimental platform for the study of large scale distributed systems. It provides over 5000 computing cores in multiple sites in France, Luxembourg and Brazil. We used a prototype of storage system implemented by a private company (Ubistorage[2]).

Our goal is to validate the main behavior of the reconstruction time in a real environment with shared and constrained bandwidth, and measure how close they are to our results.

---

[2] http://www.ubistorage.com/

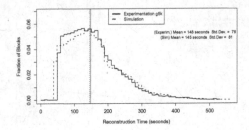

Fig. 6. Distribution of reconstruction time in an 64 nodes during 4 hours experiment compared to simulation

Storage System Description. In few words, the system is made of a storage layer (upper layer) built on top of the DHT layer (lower layer) running Pastry [13]. The lower layer is in charge of managing the logical topology: finding devices, routing, alerting of device arrivals or departures. The upper layer is in charge of storing and monitoring the data.

Storing the Data. The system uses Reed-Solomon erasure codes [15] to introduce redundancy. Each data block has a device responsible of monitoring it. This device keeps a list of the devices storing a fragment of the block. The fragments of the blocks are stored locally on the PASTRY leafset of the device in charge [16].

Monitoring the System. The storage system uses the information given by the lower level to discover device failures. In PASTRY, a device checks periodically if the members of its leafset are still up and running. When the upper layer receives a message that a device left, the device in charge updates its block status.

Monitored Metrics. The application monitors and keep statistics on the amount of data stored on its disks, the number of performed reconstructions along with their duration, the number of dead blocks that cannot be reconstructed. The upload and download bandwidth of devices can be adjusted.

Results. There exist a lot of different storage systems with different parameters and different reconstruction processes. The goal of the paper is not to precisely tune a model to a specific one, but to provide a general analytical framework to be able to predict any storage system behavior. Hence, we are more interested here by the global behavior of the metrics than by their absolute values.

Studied Scenario. By using simulations we can easily evaluate several years of a system, however it is not the case for experimentation. Time available for a simple experiment is constrained to a few hours. Hence, we define an *acceleration factor*, as the ratio between experiment duration and the time of real system we want to imitate. Our goal is to check the bandwidth congestion in a real environment. Thus, we decided to shrink the disk size (e.g., from 10 GB to 100 MB, a reduction of 100×), inducing a much smaller time to repair a failed disk. Then, the device failure rate is increased (from months to a few hours) to keep the ratio between disk failures and repair time proportional. The bandwidth limit value, however, is kept close to the one of a "real" system. The idea is to avoid inducing strange behaviors due to very small packets being transmitted in the network.

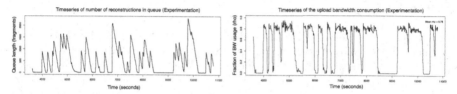

Fig. 7. Time series of the queue size (left) and the upload bandwidth ratio (right)

Figure 6 presents the distribution of the reconstruction times for two differ-ent experimentation involving 64 nodes on 2 different sites of GRID'5000. The amount of data per node is 100 MB (disk capacity 120MB), the upload band-width 128 KBps, $s = 4$, $r = 4$, $L_F = 128$ KB. We confirm that the simulator gives results very close to the one obtained by experimentation. The average value of reconstruction time differs by a few seconds.

Moreover, to have an intuition of the system dynamics over time, in Figure 7 we present a time series of the number of blocks in the queues (top plot) and the total upload bandwidth consumption (bottom plot). We note that the rate of re-constructions (the descending lines on the top plot) follows an almost linear shape. Comforting our claim that a deterministic processing time of blocks could be as-sumed. In these experiments the disk size factor is $x = 1.2$, which gives a theo-retical efficiency of 0.83. We can observe that in practice, the factor of bandwidth utilization, ρ, is very close to this value (value of $\rho = 0.78$ in the bottom plot).

6   Conclusions and Take-Aways

In this paper, we propose and analyze a new Markovian analytical model to model the repair process of distributed storage systems. This model takes into account competition for bandwidth between correlated failures. We bring to light the impact of device heterogeneity on the system efficiency. The model is validated by simulation and by real experiments on the GRID'5000 PLATFORM.

We show that load balancing in storage is crucial for reconstruction time. We introduce a simple linear factor of efficiency, where throughput of the system is divided by the ratio of maximum allowed disk size to the average occupancy.

We show that the exponential distribution, classically taken to model the reconstruction time, is valid for certain sets of parameters, but introduction of load balancing causes different shapes to appear. We show that it is not enough to be able to estimate the tail of the repair time distribution to obtain a good estimate of the data loss rate.

The results provided are for systems using Regenerating Codes that are the best codes known for bandwidth efficiency, but the model is general and can be adapted to other codes. We exhibit an interesting phenomena to keep in mind when choosing the code parameter: it is useful to keep a degree of freedom on the choice of the users participating in the repair process so that loaded or deficient users do not slow down the repair process, even if it means less efficient codes.

References

1. Valancius, V., Laoutaris, N., Massoulié, L., Diot, C., Rodriguez, P.: Greening the internet with nano data centers. In: Proceedings of the 5th International Conference on Emerging Networking Experiments and Technologies, pp. 37–48. ACM (2009)
2. Chun, B.-G., Dabek, F., Haeberlen, A., Sit, E., Weatherspoon, H., Kaashoek, M.F., Kubiatowicz, J., Morris, R.: Efficient replica maintenance for distributed storage systems. In: Proc. of USENIX NSDI, pp. 45–58 (2006)
3. Bolosky, W.J., Douceur, J.R., Ely, D., Theimer, M.: Feasibility of a serverless distributed file system deployed on an existing set of desktop PCs. ACM SIGMETRICS Perf. Eval. Review 28, 34–43 (2000)
4. Bhagwan, R., Tati, K., Chung Cheng, Y., Savage, S., Voelker, G.M.: Total recall: System support for automated availability management. In: Proc. of the USENIX NSDI, pp. 337–350 (2004)
5. Ramabhadran, S., Pasquale, J.: Analysis of long-running replicated systems. In: Proc. of IEEE INFOCOM, Spain, pp. 1–9 (2006)
6. Alouf, S., Dandoush, A., Nain, P.: Performance analysis of peer-to-peer storage systems. In: Mason, L.G., Drwiega, T., Yan, J. (eds.) ITC 2007. LNCS, vol. 4516, pp. 642–653. Springer, Heidelberg (2007)
7. Datta, A., Aberer, K.: Internet-scale storage systems under churn – a study of the steady-state using markov models. In: Procedings of the IEEE Intl. Conf. on Peer-to-Peer Computing (P2P), pp. 133–144 (2006)
8. Dandoush, A., Alouf, S., Nain, P.: Simulation analysis of download and recovery processes in P2P storage systems. In: Proc. of the Intl. Teletraffic Congress (ITC), France, pp. 1–8 (2009)
9. Picconi, F., Baynat, B., Sens, P.: Predicting durability in dhts using markov chains. In: Proceedings of the 2nd Intl. Conference on Digital Information Management (ICDIM), vol. 2, pp. 532–538 (October 2007)
10. Venkatesan, V., Iliadis, I., Haas, R.: Reliability of data storage systems under network rebuild bandwidth constraints. In: 2012 IEEE 20th International Symposium on Modeling, Analysis & Simulation of Computer and Telecommunication Systems (MASCOTS), pp. 189–197 (2012)
11. Ford, D., Labelle, F., Popovici, F.I., Stokely, M., Truong, V.-A., Barroso, L., Grimes, C., Quinlan, S.: Availability in globally distributed storage systems. In: Proceedings of the 9th USENIX Conference on Operating Systems Design and Implementation, pp. 1–7 (2010)
12. Dimakis, A., Godfrey, P., Wainwright, M., Ramchandran, K.: Network coding for distributed storage systems. In: IEEE INFOCOM, pp. 2000–2008 (May 2007)
13. Rowstron, A., Druschel, P.: Pastry: Scalable, decentralized object location, and routing for large-scale peer-to-peer systems. In: Guerraoui, R. (ed.) Middleware 2001. LNCS, vol. 2218, pp. 329–350. Springer, Heidelberg (2001)
14. Giroire, F., Gupta, S., Modrzejewski, R., Monteiro, J., Perennes, S.: Analysis of the repair time in distributed storage systems. INRIA, Research Report 7538 (February 2011)
15. Luby, M., Mitzenmacher, M., Shokrollahi, M., Spielman, D., Stemann, V.: Practical loss-resilient codes. In: Proceedings of the 29th Annual ACM Symposium on Theory of Computing, pp. 150–159 (1997)
16. Legtchenko, S., Monnet, S., Sens, P., Muller, G.: Churn-resilient replication strategy for peer-to-peer distributed hash-tables. In: Guerraoui, R., Petit, F. (eds.) SSS 2009. LNCS, vol. 5873, pp. 485–499. Springer, Heidelberg (2009)

Development and Evaluation
of a Virtual PC Type Thin Client System

Katsuyuki Umezawa, Tomoya Miyake, and Hiromi Goto

Information Technology Division, Hitachi, Ltd.,
Akihabara UDX, 14–1, Sotokanda 4-chome, Chiyoda-ku, Tokyo, 101–8010 Japan
{katsuyuki.umezawa.ue,tomoya.miyake.xh,hiromi.goto.nh}@hitachi.com
http://www.hitachi.com

Abstract. In recent years, it is thought that the virtualization of the
desktop is important as an effective solution to various problems that
a company has, such as cutting the total cost of desktop PCs that the
company owns, achieving efficiency in operative management, and having
successful security measures, compliance measures, and business continuity plans. We introduced a client blade-type thin client system, called
a "CB system," and a terminal service-type thin client system, called a
"TS system." The number of users in all of our current group companies
is approximately 70,000. We built a virtual PC-type thin client system,
called a "virtual PC system," as a new virtualization technology for the
desktop. In this paper, we give the problems we had when managing
large-scale users in a virtual PC system and suggest the solution.

Keywords: Virtualization, Thin client system, Operation management,
Load balancing.

1 Introduction

In recent years, it is thought that the virtualization of the desktop is important
as an effective solution to the various problems that a company has, such as
cutting the total cost of the desktop PCs that the company owns, achieving
efficiency in operative management, and having security measures, compliance
measures, and business continuity plans.

According to the findings of documents [2], the client virtualization solution
market, which contains the desktop virtualization solution market, in Japan in
2011 was 249,300 million yen, up 31.7% from the previous year. It spread to
372,800 million yen, up 49.5%, from 2011 in 2012. It is projected to spread
to 771,500 million yen, up 17.7%, from 2015 in 2016, and the annual average
growth rate (CAGR: Compound Annual Growth Rate) from 2011 through 2016
is predicted to be 25.3%.

We introduce a client blade type thin client system, called a "CB system," and
a terminal service type thin client system, called a "TS system." The number
of users in all of our current group companies is approximately 70,000. We built
a virtual PC type thin client system, called a "virtual PC system," as a new
virtualization technology for the desktop.

A. Hameurlain, W. Rahayu, and D. Taniar (Eds.): Globe 2013, LNCS 8059, pp. 111–123, 2013.

In this paper, we give the problems we had when managing large-scale users in a virtual PC system and suggest the solution. Specifically, we propose a method for automating the initial settings at the time when a virtual desktop is delivered to large-scale users. In addition, we propose the load dispersion method for when there are obstacles and security measures. Furthermore, we show a performance evaluation of the virtual PC system that we built, and we show how performance level improves in comparison with the CB system.

2   Classification of Desktop Virtualization Technology

Desktop virtualization technologies can be classified into CB systems, TS systems, and virtual PC systems. We show a figure of each system in figure 1.

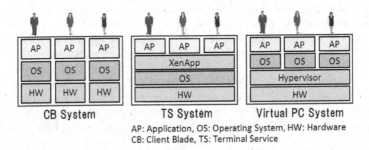

AP: Application, OS: Operating System, HW: Hardware
CB: Client Blade, TS: Terminal Service

Fig. 1. CB, TS, and Virtual PC systems

2.1   CB System

The CB system is a method for putting a thin PC, called a gblade,h in an exclusive rack. One user uses one blade. Because the CB system can install applications individually, making an environment that satisfies the needs of the user is possible. However, because computing resources are not flexible, the processing capacity may be low for a single blade; however, the processing capacity of most blades remains. In addition, managing individual client OSs can be complicated, e.g., virus measures are needed or a security patch needs to be issued to every client OS.

2.2   TS System

The TS system is a method for operating a server OS with one server and operating an application for multiple clients on a server OS. Because we can flexibly use the hardware resources of a server amongst multiple clients at the same time in a multiple desktop environment, we can make good use of them. In addition, efficient operative management is possible because we can manage applications and data intensively, but we cannot install applications individually.

2.3   Virtual PC System

The virtual PC system is a method for operating multiple virtual machines on one physical server by introducing a hypervisor and for operating an OS and desktop environment in each virtual machine. The multiple OSs operate on a server with the virtual PC system, whereas only one OS per server operates with the TS system. One virtual desktop environment operates for each individual OS. Thus, making the environment to satisfy the needs of a user is possible because we can install applications as well as CB systems individually. In addition, as well as with the TS system, we can control data intensively.

3   Summary of Our Developed Virtual PC System

We built a virtual desktop environment for 1,200 users and 5,100 users in two data centers. We plan to build a virtual desktop environment for 30,000 users in total by constructing three data centers, each for 10,000 users, in the future.

We show some configurations of the system that we built in figure 2. As is shown, the virtual desktop copes with hardware obstacles by assuming a high availability (HA) configuration of 15:1. In addition, we made redundant the authentication server, virtual desktop deploy server, virtual desktop login server, and the scan definition server by using Active-Active configurations in order to deal with load dispersion and obstacles. We made the file server redundant by using N+1 configurations to save it for obstacle measures. We made some storage management servers in accordance with the number required to manage the system.

In addition, we show the function of each server shown in figure 2 in table 1. Furthermore, we show the procedure detailed in table 2 for when a user logs into their own virtual desktop in figure 2.

4   Operative Problem and Solution to Large-Scale Virtual PC System

When we manage a large-scale virtual PC system, the following problems become clear.

- How can we effectively deploy a virtual desktop to a large number of users?
- How can we avoid obstacles and load balancing when security measures are used?

4.1   Deploy Method Proposal

The virtual desktop delivery server delivers individual virtual desktops on a hypervisor. This process is carried out by manual labor while referring to necessary information, which is given by a manager. Specifically, a manager must set various pieces of information such as the fixed IP address or the license key, which

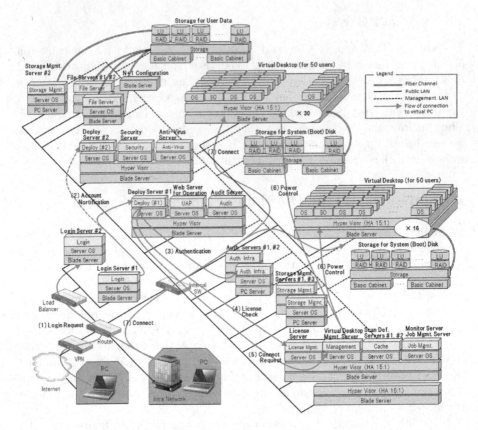

Fig. 2. Summary of Virtual PC System

are necessary when operating a virtual desktop on an OS as needed. Therefore, setup becomes difficult when the number of virtual desktops becomes large (e.g., tens of thousands).

In this section, we propose a method for carrying out the initial settings for deploying many virtual desktops effectively.

Configuration of System for Deployment. We show the configuration of the system used for deploying the virtual desktops that we proposed in figure 3. As shown in the figure, the proposed system comprises a deploy management server, a deploy server, a blade server, and a DHCP server.

Here, the deploy server should adopt an existing technique. In addition, the DHCP server is necessary in order to give the necessary IP address when a virtual desktop deployed on a hypervisor communicates with a deploy management server first.

Table 1. Explanation of Each Server in Fig. 2

Server Name	Function
Storage Mgmt. Server	Manages storage
File Server	Stores personal data such as the desktop information for every user
Deploy Server	Deploys the virtual desktop and links with the user
Security Server	Manages security patches
Anti-Virus Server	Collectively manages anti-virus software
Web Server for Operation	Web page on the virtual PC system
Audit Server	Manages audits and settings of the virtual PC
Auth. Server	Manages user account info and rights
Virtual Desktop Mgmt. Server	Manages hypervisor and virtual desktop
License Server	Manages licenses
Scan Def. Server	Maintains the cash information of the virus scan
Monitor Server	Automatically monitors event viewer information of the server
Job Mgmt. Server	Provides automation functions for the server maintenance
Login Server	Provides functions for logging in to a virtual desktop

Table 2. User Login Procedure in Fig. 2

(1) Login Request	Connect by using the connection software of the PC
(2) Account Notification	Send LDAP information
(3) Authentication	Authenticate by using LDAP information.
(4) License Check	Check the number of virtual desktop connections
(5) Connect Request	Request connection to an applicable virtual desktop
(6) Power Control	Confirm the state of the connection and switch it to "on" if cut off
(7) Connect	Send LDAP and digital certificate and connect

Processing Flow at Time of Deployment. We show the processing flows of initialization after having deployed a virtual desktop. We show the flow of the virtual desktop at the time of deployment in figure 4.

First, the deploy management server transmits deploy instructions (datastore information and host name set beforehand) to a deploy server depending on the instructions of the operator. The deploy server carries out deployment on the basis of the datastore information and the host name included in the deploy instructions. The hypervisor deploys a virtual desktop in an appointed datastore and host name and outputs a deploy result to the deploy server. The host name and physical address of the virtual desktop that was deployed are included in this deploy result. The deploy server keeps it as a deploy result.

Then, the deploy management server transmits the host name to a deploy server and acquires the physical address of the virtual desktop that got the correspondence in a host name. The deploy management server keeps a physical address with the host name.

The deployed virtual desktop starts by following the start instructions from the hypervisor and acquires the temporary IP address from a DHCP server. The virtual desktop transmits its own physical address to a deploy management server and acquires the setting information (host name, fixed IP address, the license keys of the operating system, etc.) afterwards. The virtual desktop sets those pieces of information and reboots.

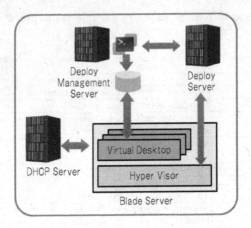

Fig. 3. System for Deploying Virtual Desktop

Thus, in accordance with the proposed method, the process for deploying a large number of virtual client environments is automated.

4.2 Proposal of Load Balancing during Use

The measures mentioned above are a proposal to simplify the initial settings for a large number of users. In this section, we propose load balancing for when we apply various processes such as updating the OS, the security patches, and virus scans in multiple numerical virtual desktops after the deployment.

Load Balancing by One to One Grouping. Figure 5 is an example of load balancing by mapping a blade and a storage unit one to one.

We assign multiple (e.g., 40–60) virtual desktops on one hypervisor to an individual datastore. Thus, virtual desktops on different hypervisors do not share the same datastore. Because a virtual desktop on a certain hypervisor is not affected by the virtual desktop on other hypervisors when we update the OS and application or do a virus scan, we can realize load balancing.

However, for example, this assumes there is an obstacle to the blade server on which there is one hypervisor and that the blade server is restored by the HA configuration (dualization) automatically. In this case, the problem remains that the load concentrates on one storage because disk I/O occurs from all virtual desktops on one hypervisor at the same time.

Load Balancing by Meshed Grouping. Figure 6 is an example of load balancing that improved the configuration that we showed in figure 5.

We disperse and assign each virtual desktop on one hypervisor to multiple datastores in order to plan for dispersion of the network load between a hypervisor and the datastore in this proposal. Unlike the configuration of figure 5, the

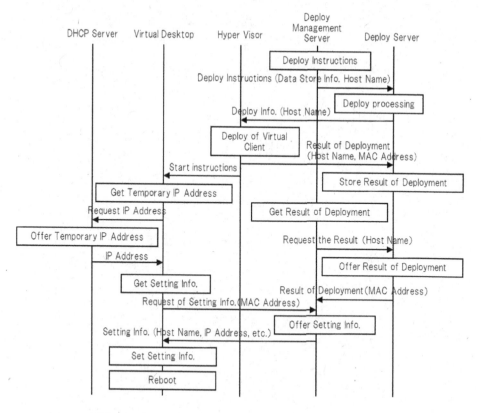

Fig. 4. Flow at Time of Deploying Virtual Desktop

blade servers on which there is one hypervisor can disperse the load of the disk I/O if we assume that the hypervisor can do so when an obstacle occurs.

Load Balancing by Grouping for Management. Figure 7 is a configuration that is an improved version of the one that we showed in figure 6. The network configuration between a hypervisor and the datastore is similar to that in the figure 6.

When we update the OS and applications or do a virus scan with this proposal, grouping is performed on each virtual desktop on the hypervisor that does not share a datastore. The deploy management server gives instructions to one (or a few) group unit.

In accordance with this proposal, processing is carried out for every group. In one group, only a few virtual desktops on one hypervisor share a datastore. Thus, we can plan for the dispersion of the network load between the hypervisor and the datastore better.

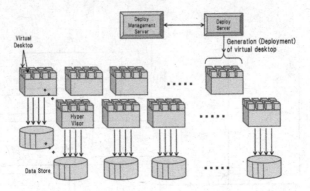

Fig. 5. One to One Grouping

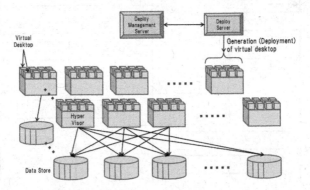

Fig. 6. Grouping by Generating Mesh

5   Evaluation

5.1   Evaluation of Proposed Method

About Proposed Deploy Method. We have deployed the virtual desktop for several thousand users so far. Under the present conditions, we can deploy approximately ten virtual desktops in an hour (we can become parallel). In addition, most of this time is the time that the desktop environment takes to deploy itself. We think that the effect of the automation is sufficient.

About Load Balancing by Meshed Mapping. Several hardware obstacles have happened so far. However, the system that encountered an obstacle was a system made before taking measures to balance the load by meshed mapping. Evaluating the effects of this load balancing is a future goal.

About Load Balancing by Grouping for Management. We performed the grouping that we proposed at the time of updating the OS and applications and delivering the definition file of the virus scan. In the past, the disorder that the load of the disk I/O soared occurred without grouping having been performed due to incorrect settings. However, we can now avoid this remarkable rise of disk I/O by using appropriate grouping.

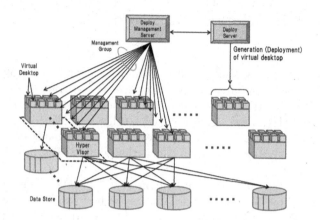

Fig. 7. Load Balancing by Grouping for Management

5.2   Performance Evaluation of the System That We Built

Objective of Performance Evaluation. Because a virtual PC system is a system with which a user uses multiple servers at the same time, evaluating the performance is necessary. The virtual PC system shares one storage unit with multiple users. Because the OSs are stored in a common storage unit, the increase of the disk I/O time has a big influence on the user experience during operation. Therefore, in this section, we pay our attention to a value, the current disk queue length, which is an index of the disk performance, and we perform a performance evaluation.

Performance Evaluation Method. First, (1) we find two load level standard values (in normal load and in peak load) from the actual value of the conventional system (CB system). (2) We make a load tool that produces an equal load. (3) We measure how well the system operates while giving a pseudo load with the load tool to each of the virtual desktop environments for 50 users, 55 users, and 60 users on one server of the virtual PC system[1]. We show items for evaluating how well the system operated in table 3.

---

[1] With the configuration of the proposed system, the load of one storage depends on the number of users on one hypervisor. Therefore, an evaluation with 40-60 users is sufficient enough.

Table 3. Items for Performance Evaluation

#	Evaluating time	Details
1	Logon	OS boot time [sec]
2	Application boot	Boot time of Excel 2007, Word 2007, PowerPoint 2007, and PDF [sec]
3	Operation response	Scroll time of Excel 2007, Word 2007, PowerPoint 2007, and PDF [sec]
4	Browser indication	Indication time of Internet Explorer 8 [sec]

Determination of Standard Load Value. In documents [15][16][17], the method for managing resources in the virtualization technology of the desktop is discussed. Particularly, it is stated in these documents [15][16] that the CPU utilization in one day is associated with each other day. We confirmed that the current disk queue length, which is an index of the performance of the disk I/O, repeats itself periodically by using a correlation analysis like in the documents [15][16].

Therefore, we paid our attention to more detailed data (every ten minutes) for one day. We show detailed data for one day in figure 8. The cross axis shows the time. The vertical axis shows the mean of the current disk queue length of 20 users who used the CB system.

We understand that a singular point is in the neighborhood of 9:00, 13:00, and 19:00 from figure 8. Thus, we defined 30 minutes before and after a singular point as the peak load time and the others as a normal load time. We calculated the peak load value as the maximum peak load time and the normal load value for the mean as the normal load time. We calculated the highest value of each load value for the standard value of the peak and normal load as a representative. As a result, the peak load level became 2.43 from 8:30 to 9:30, and the normal load value became 0.28 from 9:30 to 12:30.

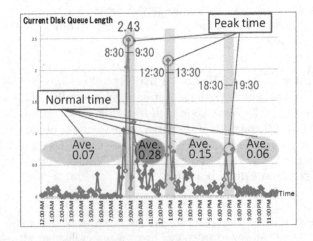

Fig. 8. Transition of Load for One Day

In addition, for the load mean from 9:30 to 12:30 from Monday to Friday, it was examined daily by using a one way layout analysis that there was a variance of 5% for the levels of significance, indicating that there was not a difference between days of the week.

Making of Load Tool. We made a tool for executing the process shown below repeatedly and gave a pseudo load.

- Reading and writing Excel and Word files.
- Reading and scrolling through PowerPoint and PDF files.
- Reading a web page with Internet Explorer.

We used this tool with a conventional CB system and adjusted it to agree with the load level that we found in the previous section.

Inspecting User Experience. We show inspection results for the normal load on the left side of table 4. For the evaluation items, which we showed in table 3, we show the ratio of the evaluation result of the virtual PC system to the evaluation result with the conventional CB system. If a value is smaller than 100%, it means that the system is faster than the CB system; otherwise, it means that it is slower than the CB system. We were able to confirm the following things from table 4.

- The processing time was not affected by the number of users if the number was within 40 - 60 users.
- In comparison with the CB system, processing time was shortened by approximately 50%.

Table 4. Results of Performance Evaluation

Evaluating time	Normal time			Peak time		
	50 users	55 users	60 users	50 users	55 users	60 users
Logon	61%	61%	66%	63%	63%	66%
Application boot	42%	43%	43%	133%	211%	275%
Operation response	54%	54%	54%	100%	102%	102%
Browser indication	53%	42%	46%	162%	167%	146%

We show the result of the performance evaluation in the peak load on the right side of table 4. It was approximately 60%, 100%, and 150% for logon, operation response, and browser indication time, respectively. For application boot-time, it became 133%, 211%, 275% for 50 users, 55 users, and 60 users, respectively. For processing without the logon, we needed more than 100% of processing time. However, we think that the result for the peak hour is within a tolerable range because the peak hour was limited only to approximately ten minutes of the morning.

6   Related Work

Some works [3][4][5] focus on latency and bandwidth between the thin client system and server, and a number of research projects [6][7][8][9][10][12] consider VM placement models. Other researchers [11] have studied the performance of storage in virtualized environments. However, the above works are not in the context of virtual desktops.

Regarding virtual desktops, a resource defragmentation algorithm based on virtual desktop migration is presented in [13], and a resource allocation model based on the benchmarking tool is presented in [14]. The method for managing resources in the virtualization technology of the desktop is discussed in [15][16][17]. Particularly, it is stated that the CPU utilization in one day is associated with each other day in [15][16]. The method for reducing the load on shared storage by using caches is presented in [18][19]. In this paper, we evaluated the work load of virtual desktops by using the technique described in [15][16].

7   Conclusion and Future Work

We proposed a method for solving a problem when managing large-scale users in a virtual PC system. The proposals are automating the initial settings at the time of deployment and using a load dispersion method for when obstacle and security measures are taken. In addition, we showed a performance evaluation of the virtual PC system. We were able to show that the performance level improved in comparison with the conventional system (CB system) by reviewing the evaluation result. It will be necessary to carry out a similar test in a real environment and to reevaluate the user experience during operation in the future.

About Trademarks

- Microsoft, Excel, Word, PowerPoint, and Internet Explorer are registered trademarks of the Microsoft Corporation in the U.S.A and other countries.

References

1. ITOCHU Techno-Solutions Corporation, VMware vSphere Enterprise Integration, SHOEISHA (2010)
2. Japan client virtualization market prediction, International Data Corporation Japan (2012), http://www.idcjapan.co.jp/Press/Current/20120607Apr.html
3. Lai, A., Nieh, J.: On the performance of widearea thin-client computing. ACM Transactions on Computer Systems, 175–209 (2006)
4. Tolia, N., Andersen, D.G., Satyanarayanan, M.: Quantifying interactive user experience on thin clients. IEEE Computer 39, 46–52 (2006)
5. Berryman, A., Calyam, P., Lai, A., Honigford, M.: Vdbench: A benchmarking toolkit for thinclient based virtual desktop environments. In: The 2nd IEEE International Conference on Cloud Computing Technology and Science (CloudCom), pp. 480–487. EEE (2010)

6. Malet, B., Pietzuch, P.: Resource allocation across multiple cloud data centres. In: 8th International Workshop on Middleware for Grids, Clouds and e-Science (MGC) (2010)
7. Mohammadi, E., Karimi, M., Heikalabad, S.: A novel virtual machine placement in cloud computing. Australian Journal of Basic and Applied Sciences 5, 1549–1555 (2011)
8. Piao, J.T., Yan, J.: A network-aware virtual machine placement and migration approach in cloud computing. In: Ninth International Conference on Grid and Cloud Computing, pp. 87–92 (2010)
9. Sonnek, J., Greensky, J., Reutiman, R., Chandra, A.: Starling: minimizing communication overhead in virtualized computing platforms using decentralized affinity-aware migration. In: The 39th International Conference on Parallel Processing (ICPP), pp. 228–237 (2010)
10. Sato, K., Sato, H., Matsuoka, S.: A model-based algorithm for optimizing io intensive applications in clouds using vm-based migration. In: IEEE/ACM International Symposium on Cluster Computing and the Grid (CCGRID), pp. 466–471 (2009)
11. Gulati, A., Kumar, C., Ahmad, I.: Storage workload characterization and consolidation in virtualized environments. In: 2nd International Workshop on Virtualization Performance: Analysis, Characterization, and Tools (VPACT) (2009)
12. Zhang, Z., Xiao, L., Li, Y., Ruan, L.: A VM-based Resource Management Method Using Statistics. In: 2012 IEEE 18th International Conference on Parallel and Distributed Systems, icpads, pp. 788–793 (2012)
13. Shridharan, M., Calyam, P., Venkataraman, A., Berryman, A.: Defragmentation of resources in virtual desktop clouds for cost-aware utility optimal allocation. In: Fourth IEEE International Conference on Utility and Cloud Computing, pp. 253–260 (2011)
14. Calyam, P., Patali, R., Berryman, A., Lai, A.M., Ramnath, R.: Utility-directed resource allocation in virtual desktop clouds. The International Journal of Computer and Telecommunications Networking 55, 4112–4130 (2011)
15. Lethanhman, C., Kayashima, M.: Virtual Machine Placement Algorithm for Virtualized Desktop Infrastructure. In: Proceedings of IEEE CCISC 2011 (2011)
16. Le Thanh Man, C., Kayashima, M.: Desktop Work Load Characteristics and Their Utility in Optimizing Virtual Machine Placement in Cloud. In: Proceedings of IEEE CCISC 2012 (2012)
17. Kochut, A., Beaty, K., Shaikh, H., Shea, D.G.: Desktop Workload Study with Implications for Desktop Cloud Resource Optimization. In: Proceedings of IEEE International Symposium on IPDPSWC 2010 (2010)
18. Shamma, M., Meyer, D.T., Wires, J., Ivanova, M., Hutchinson, N.C., Warfield, A.: Capo: Recapitulating Storage for Virtual Desktops. In: Proceedings of 9th USENIX Conference on File and Storage Technologies, pp. 31–45 (2011)
19. Lagar-Cavilla, H., Whitney, J., Scannell, A., Patchin, P., Rumble, S., De Lara, E., Brudno, M., Satyanarayanan, M.: SnowFlock: rapid virtual machine cloning for cloud computing. In: Proceedings of the 4th ACM European Conference on Computer Systems, pp. 1–12 (2009)

Author Index

Agrawal, Divyakant 1
Akbarinia, Reza 1
Albert, Erik 75
Ali, Liaquat 63
Alshabani, Amjad 39

Baude, Françoise 39
Bellatreche, Ladjel 13
Bouchakri, Rima 13

Chawathe, Sudarshan S. 75
Cuzzocrea, Alfredo 13

Damigos, Matthew 51
Defude, Bruno 87

Gergatsoulis, Manolis 51
Giroire, Frédéric 99
Goto, Hiromi 111
Grov, Jon 26
Gupta, Sandeep Kumar 99

Huet, Fabrice 39

Janson, Thomas 63

Kalogeros, Eleftherios 51

Lausen, Georg 63
Liroz-Gistau, Miguel 1

Maabout, Sofian 13
Miyake, Tomoya 111
Modrzejewski, Remigiusz 99
Monteiro, Julian 99

Nomikos, Christos 51

Ölveczky, Peter Csaba 26

Pacitti, Esther 1
Pellegrino, Laurent 39
Perennes, Stéphane 99

Schindelhauer, Christian 63
Sellami, Rami 87

Umezawa, Katsuyuki 111

Valduriez, Patrick 1